THE SLACKER'S GUIDE TO

D0644239

U.S. HISTORY

The Bare Minimum on Discovering America,
the Boston Tea Party, the California Gold Rush,
and Lots of Other Stuff Dead White Guys Did

DON STEWART AND JOHN PFEIFFER

Adamsmedia

Avon, Massachusetts

Published by
Adams Media, a division of F+W Media, Inc.
57 Littlefield Street, Avon, MA 02322. U.S.A.
www.adamsmedia.com

ISBN 10: 1-60550-346-0
ISBN 13: 978-1-60550-346-2

Printed in the United States of America.

J I H G F E D C B A

Library of Congress Cataloging-in-Publication Data
is available from the publisher.

This publication is designed to provide accurate and authoritative information
with regard to the subject matter covered. It is sold with the understanding that
the publisher is not engaged in rendering legal, accounting, or other professional
advice. If legal advice or other expert assistance is required, the services of a competent professional person should be sought.

—From a *Declaration of Principles* jointly adopted by a Committee of the
American Bar Association and a Committee of Publishers and Associations

Many of the designations used by manufacturers and sellers to distinguish their
product are claimed as trademarks. Where those designations appear in this book
and Adams Media was aware of a trademark claim, the designations have been
printed with initial capital letters.

This book is available at quantity discounts for bulk purchases.
For information, please call 1-800-289-0963.

ACKNOWLEDGMENTS

Don Stewart's Acknowledgments

A huge thank you goes out to my unbelievably supportive wife Erin. You have shown me time and time again what unconditional love is even when I have probably deserved love with a handful of conditions attached to it.

An equally huge thank you goes out to my two incredible kids, Emma and Joshua. Even though it will be years before you will be allowed to read this book, I want you to know how much I love the two of you.

To my parents Don and Dianne, thank you for the lifetime of love you have given me and the opportunities that you worked so hard to provide me with.

To my in-laws Bob and Blair, thank you for all of the times you have gone above and beyond to show your support to me. It is very much appreciated and will never be forgotten.

To Meredith O'Hayre of Adams Media, thanks for all of your hard work and enthusiasm for this project. John and I are fortunate to have had the opportunity to work with you on this book.

To Steve Harris of CSG Literary Partners, LLC for representing this book. You took a chance on us and we are grateful that you did.

And finally, thank you to the rest of my family and friends. Your encouragement during the writing of this book was been invaluable.

Thanks again to everyone.

John Pfeiffer's Acknowledgements

Don and I have just wrapped on the final touches of writing *Slacker's Guide*. As I type the last word, I do the double chest pound with my fist and then point to the sky a la Deion Sanders. Don and I attempt to do the flying chestbump, but we barely achieve liftoff, and both end up injured. While I am on the disabled list (out of shape, day-to-day), I wanted to take time to give thanks where it is due.

I want to thank and send love to my wife Alana, who had faith in me (and the project) when there was no reason to have any. A shout out goes to my three girls: Kaitlyn, Lindsay, and Zoey, who put up with me and my sense of humor on a daily basis. To our agent Steve Harris, who took a chance on us and our dirty history book. To Adams Media, for giving first-time authors a chance. Big ups to Meredith O'Hayre, for her guidance through the process and tact in reining us in when we needed it. HUGE thanks to Bonnie Hearn Hill, who taught us how to query and write a proposal, and mentally prepared us for the wave of rejection that was to follow. Props and love to the DAFL and WWL, for wasting my time when I should have been writing. Thanks to John Mueller, who was invaluable to me, and was there for me literally every step of the way. To my Mother, who I am sure is looking down at this project and hopefully chuckling. Thanks goes to Roy and Marie and Ken and Joan, for being so supportive in so many areas of my life. Special thanks to Bob and Melinda, Doug and Chantel, Wendy and Wayne, and Megan and Jeff for your all-purpose awesomeness and not laughing (at least to my face) when I told you Don and I were going to write a book. Peace and I'm out.

CONTENTS

Introduction . . . ix

INTRODUCTION

Warning!

The following passage is for illustrative purposes only. It is in no way a reflection of the authors' philosophy on American history. In fact, the purpose of this paragraph is to emphasize what is wrong with the current crop of books published about U.S. history. If for any reason while reading this illustrative paragraph, you suffer from shortness of breath, sweaty palms, or an overwhelming desire to seek out the worm at the bottom of a tequila bottle, calmly stop reading and proceed to the next paragraph. Please note: The following paragraph has been borrowed in its entirety from Edward Channing. Mr. Channing is a Harvard history professor and the author of *A Short History of the United States*. What follows is from the first paragraph of the preface of his book. Again, proceed with caution!

> *"The study of the history of one's own country is a serious matter, and should be entered upon by the text-book writer, by the teacher, and by the pupil in a serious spirit, even to a greater extent than the study of language or of arithmetic. . . . It is a text-book pure and simple, and should be used as a text-book, to be studied diligently by the pupil and expounded carefully by the teacher."*

Wow. Is it any wonder no one is getting a hard-on for history at Harvard?

Unfortunately, this is the type of philosophy that is embedded in nearly every book ever published about American history. As a result, it is not only the students of Harvard who can't seem to get it stiff for history, but also the rest of the country. People who write about history tend to take the subject matter and themselves way too seriously.

The stuffy history professor with a half dozen initials after his name who is popping double stacks of Viagra between lectures is not qualified to write a book like this. The slacker generation has been tuning out these talking heads for years. They have sat in lecture halls with their fellow collegiate comrades trying to decide whether it's Dr. Talking Head, MLS soccer, or a preseason WNBA game that has the greater power to suck your soul dry. Unfortunately, for most, the conclusion was Dr. Talking Head.

Syllabus

Please read through the following syllabus at your convenience. There is no need to rush through the material, as this course is not designed for over-achievers. There will be no extra credit for students who exceed expectations. The performance expectations for this course have been set very low. Please make no effort to impress us with high test scores and well-written essays. Any student who is willing to screw up the bell curve for the rest of the class by scoring outrageously high marks will be promptly dismissed from this course, as this behavior is considered unacceptable.

Course Objectives: The purpose of this course is to prove that American history is flat-out funny when it is retold by us. We don't care if you're eight or eighty, blind, crippled or crazy, we want to tell *you* our version of U.S. history.

Prerequisites: A pulse, a sense of humor, and $12.95 to purchase your course book, *The Slacker's Guide to U.S. History*. Literacy is optional.

Course Description: This course will cover the most significant events in U.S. history. Lesser events have been ignored in order to give us the opportunity to explore the important subtopics of presidential infidelity, all-night benders, gambling, and adult dancers. Please check any preconceived notions that history is boring at the door.

Course Expectations: By the end of this course, you should be able to answer the following questions:

1. If you and a friend were left for dead in the middle of the Cherokee National Forest, would you want that friend to be Meriwether Lewis, Jennifer Aniston, or Trapper John MD?
2. If in December 1917 Congress had voted to hand out "Just Say No to Booze" buttons in high schools throughout the country instead of passing Prohibition legislation, would Americans drink less booze today?
3. Has Al Gore gone Hollywood?
4. If you had to choose between the following sets of past and present political leaders to anchor your U.S. Political Rotisserie team, who would you choose: Andrew Jackson, Franklin D. Roosevelt, and Condoleezza Rice; Woodrow Wilson, Gerald Ford, and Colin Powell; or Thomas Jefferson, Harry S. Truman, and Hillary Clinton?
5. As it is currently constructed, does the Republican Party qualify as a cult?

Examinations

There will be three exams, each consisting of easy multiple-choice questions along with the always-popular fifty-fifty-chance true/false questions. If any one test score is less than desirable, we allow for one mulligan, so use it wisely. Under no circumstances is a student to prepare for a test by studying previously covered material. Studying is tantamount to cheating. Cramming your ass off the night before does not accurately reflect what you have learned. Taking an exam without studying is a true indication of what you know on the day of the exam and what you will know three months later. Any student caught studying will automatically receive a failing grade, no exceptions.

All grading will be based on pass/fail. We find this helps to contain and frustrate overachievers.

Closing Thought

Upon successful completion of the course material, you will immediately go buy another copy of *The Slacker's Guide to U.S. History* and give it to somebody who hates you. The goodwill that is spread along with the laughter will eventually bring about world peace, or at the very least, end the border skirmishes we are experiencing with Canada and Mexico.

1492

COLUMBUS DISCOVERS AMERICA

The Spanish royals gave him the equivalent of two bathtubs and a rowboat . . .

GIRL YOU KNOW IT'S TRUE (G-G-G-IRL)

Most Americans who choose to pursue a job within the government or in the banking industry decide to commit their working hours to one of these enterprises for a very simple reason. Over the years, the vast majority of companies across the country have recklessly and deliberately phased out perhaps the most sacred of all our holidays, the celebration of Christopher Columbus's discovery of the New World. What should be a statutory day of excessive exuberance that ends in public drunkenness is now ignored by nearly all private employers. ☞ *This gap in the October party schedule has proven to be unacceptable to many, resulting in scores of job seekers intentionally limiting their available employment opportunities to banks and government to keep this treasured holiday on their calendar.* ✑

Dream Weaver

A sailor of above average talents, Christopher Columbus was born in the trendy Italian seaport of Genoa. He was the son of a wool merchant and wool weaver. Despite the glamour involved in the wool industry, he had dreams that only a vast ocean and a boat full of men could live up to.

Columbus dreamed of proving to those still in doubt that the world was in fact round by sailing confidently due west to reach the Spice Lands recognized as valuable trading outposts for European monarchs. For Columbus, the problem with proving the doubters wrong was that the trickle-down from a wool merchant was embarrassingly small, leaving him with very little start-up capital of his own. Discouraged but not beaten, Columbus began to solicit venture capital from government-backed programs.

The Portuguese quickly rejected his application, believing that Columbus's assumptions concerning the circumference of the Earth were unrealistic and shortsighted. But like all good sons of wool weavers, Columbus did not allow this initial rejection to defeat him. Instead, he dusted off his best suit and threw on his favorite playboy bunny tie and traveled to Spain, to spin his yarn about the world to King Ferdinand V and Queen Isabella. ☞ *Although he was initially rejected again, his annoying persistence finally paid off when the Spanish royals gave him the equivalent of two bathtubs and a rowboat, which were promptly named the **Santa Maria**, the **Niña**, and the **Pinta**.* ☜ With his nearly seaworthy fleet in hand, Columbus and ninety somewhat reluctant men set sail to the west in April 1492.

One Big Discovery, Mon

After drifting west for more than a month, everyone on the subpar vessels started wondering whether Columbus was in need of a code red, Portuguese

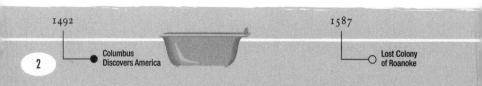

1492

Columbus
Discovers America

1587

Lost Colony
of Roanoke

style. The crappy food, smelly shipmates, and lack of knowledge with respect to their whereabouts had lost its intrigue weeks ago. Sensing a thorough beating on the horizon, Columbus guessed southwest, and in the early morning of October 12, land was sighted. As they landed on an island in the Bahamas, the natives were caught off guard. Surprised to have visitors this late in the tourist season, the locals offered to braid the sailors' hair and sell them cheap rum. Instead of thanking them for their hospitality, the always polite white visitors offered to enslave them.

After much consideration and debate, Columbus named the island San Salvador, and over the next few weeks he landed at what are now known as Cuba, the Dominican Republic, and Haiti. Columbus, always the eternal optimist, believed he had proven that the world was in fact round.

The Real Deal Holyfield

Over the years, private businesses have hired scores of lobbyists to discredit Columbus's recognition for discovering the New World in an effort to justify their unwillingness to allow their employees to participate in Columbus Day shenanigans. Frequent mailers and radio ads point to Leif Erickson exploring the North American coastline over 500 years earlier. Regardless of the facts, many people still feel that the month of October deserves a party, and they feel comfortable using Christopher Columbus as the reason for it.

1587

THE LOST COLONY OF ROANOKE

…it would be easy for his free-spirited family to land American green cards and give them a Disney Fast Pass to citizenship.

Green Card up Their Sleeve

Long before poor and desperate Mexican parents began smuggling their pregnant daughters into the United States in an attempt to secure American citizenship for all of their underachieving family members, John White, an English-born artist, was writing the "illegal alien to full citizen in three easy steps!" playbook. Receiving the blessing of Queen Elizabeth I, White brought his pregnant daughter Eleanor to the New World. White was ecstatic to learn that his daughter got knocked-up by a hometown brick-layer named Ananias Dare. He reasoned that if Eleanor's bundle of joy was born on what would soon become U.S. soil, with the lack of immigration regulations in the New World, ☞ *it would be easy for his free-spirited family to land American green cards and give them a Disney Fast Pass to citizenship.* ▨

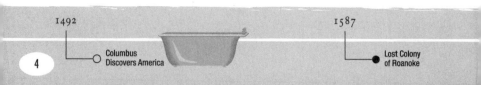

1492
Columbus
Discovers America

1587
Lost Colony
of Roanoke

4

Once the "Settlers Wanted" poster went up in the town square, White put his pregnant daughter and son-in-law's names at the top of the list. Leaning on his favorable relationship with the queen, White managed to be appointed governor of the new settlement.

White was aware that there had been an earlier attempt to establish a British colony in the area in 1585, however, it failed when the fifteen settlers pleaded with a ship returning to England to give them passage back to the comforts of their own country. Many British historians argue that these original settlers must have been French, not English, because of how quickly and easily they surrendered.

Spanglish Conflict

In July 1587, the 117 handpicked men, woman, and children stormed the shores of Roanoke Island. Celebrating their safe arrival in the New World, the settlers gave the Indians their first taste of British hooliganism, yelling "Real Madrid sucks" while running half naked along the shores of Roanoke Island and setting random fires. The Native Americans were left questioning how long they really wanted this group of strangers to remain their neighbors on what was once a peaceful sliver of paradise.

Benefiting from his position as governor, White convinced his rowdy group of settlers that it would be in the best interest of the colony if he returned to England to acquire more supplies. With the blessing of the settlers, White boarded his ship and headed back to England promising to return in three months loaded with everything a struggling settler could ever want.

Unfortunately for the settlers left behind, the Spanish and English governments decided to play a game centered around who could kill more men in uniform and citizens from the other team. As the road team, the Spanish were forced to make the long journey to England. ☞ *DESPITE being listed AS*

1619 1620   1626

Slavery Comes
to America   The Pilgrims Land   Purchase of
                    on Plymouth Rock   Manhattan

GOING
OUT OF
BUSINESS

5

heavy favorites by both Las Vegas and off-shore casinos, the Spanish were defeated two years later. ➡ With the fun and games over, White headed back to those he wished to govern again.

Which Way Did They Go?

Arriving back in Roanoke nearly three years after he left, White expected to see the colony flourishing. Unfortunately, when he arrived he found no soccer pitches, no newspaper tabloids, and more importantly no one who spoke with an accent similar to his. In fact, the only signs that life had ever existed in the area were a couple of government-subsidized huts that were falling apart, as government housing often does, and the word CROATOAN carved into a large tree.

The search for the missing settlers has been ongoing for the last 400 years. Although most people involved in the search and rescue operation believe it is unlikely any of the original settlers will be found alive, they continue to look, hoping to provide answers for the families of the missing. Over the years, there have been many theories as to what happened to the settlers, including death by Ethiopian-like starvation, death by hurricane, and death by Indian. Perhaps the most probable scenario was that they were enticed farther into the mainland by the possibility of hot and spicy Anglo/Indian love. With the colony gone and his daughter and citizenship-ticket granddaughter missing, White abandoned his earlier green card seeking behavior and chose against becoming an undocumented alien and returned to England, never realizing his dream of American citizenship.

1492
Columbus
Discovers America

1587
Lost Colony
of Roanoke

1619

SLAVERY COMES TO AMERICA

Hours were long, benefits were nonexistent, and office beatings were common

Coming to America

It took twelve years for the white Euro settlers to realize that building a country from its roots could not be done on the backs of those whose complexion was similar to that of George Clooney and Leonardo DiCaprio. Instead, it needed to be accomplished by volunteers who looked more like Denzel Washington and Will Smith. Using the resources of well-connected Dutch slave traders, the men of Jamestown, Virginia, placed an order for twenty hardworking black men, who were enthusiastic about working on labor-intensive farms while enduring brutal beatings by those they yearned to call "Master."

1619 1620   1626

Slavery Comes to America   The Pilgrims Land on Plymouth Rock   Purchase of Manhattan

GOING OUT OF BUSINESS

Not as Good as Advertised

Slavery was not the state of utopia that you might suspect. ☞ *Long hours, no pay, and being treated like property did not make for an easy living.* ☜ After being yanked from the Motherland you could be separated from your family on a whim, and your white master could decide he wanted to see if your wife's legendary bedroom skills were what he was looking for. The hours were long, the benefits were almost nonexistent, and office beatings were common. But from an altruistic standpoint, your hard labor was the backbone of the economy in the Southern states, which you should have felt good about.

Slavery—the Dark Meat on America's Thanksgiving Turkey

The idea of using slave labor fit nicely into the business plans of America's first farmers. Like many businesses, high labor costs and soaring health insurance made it difficult to turn a profit. By using slave labor almost exclusively, a farm owner's operating costs were reduced significantly, and the need to pay FICA taxes could be overlooked. These savings could be passed on to the farmer's wife and kids. More importantly, the slaves themselves could be passed on to the farmer's wife and kids. The descendants of rich slave farmers should give thanks every year for the bounty provided to them by somewhat underappreciated slaves.

Seeing how effective their new human property was working out on their farms' balance sheets, nearly every farmer's expansion plans included the purchase of new and equally enthusiastic slaves. Over the next several decades the slave labor market grew to nearly 4 million brothers and sisters in bondage. With so many slaves hitting the job market so quickly, many

1587
Lost Colony
of Roanoke

1619
Slavery Comes
to America

were forced to post their resume on CareerBuilder.com. Many Africans who had experience in tobacco and cotton hoped to further their slaving careers in growth states like Alabama, Mississippi, and Texas. This realignment of slave talent made life easier on whites in these areas, and changed the landscape of Popeye's franchises forever.

1620

The Pilgrims Land
on Plymouth Rock

1626

Purchase of
Manhattan

GOING
OUT OF
BUSINESS

1681

Pennsylvania
and the Quakers

9

1620

THE PILGRIMS LAND ON PLYMOUTH ROCK

As the 102 settlers collectively broke out singing The Soup Dragons' version of "I'm Free," a star was born.

A Rocky Road

The now famous castoffs who fled British harassment and bad beer on the mostly seaworthy *Mayflower* vessel disappointedly landed on Plymouth Rock in 1620. Far removed from the British monarchy's line of succession, William Bradford assembled a tight-knit group of members from the Separatist sect of British Protestantism along with a number of not-so-God-fearing additional fare paying passengers on their voyage in order to make the trip financially feasible.

Bradford's group called themselves "Saints," and (keeping in mind that their God was better than everyone else's God) they named the rest of the passengers "Strangers." With the Strangers threatening mutiny and a brutal winter approaching, the "let's be more civil to each other" Mayflower Compact

1587 — Lost Colony of Roanoke

1619 Slavery Comes to America

1620 The Pilgrims Land on Plymouth Rock

was drawn up to help the two groups work out their differences in the name of mutual survival.

☞ *DESPITE THEIR FUNNY ACCENTS AND BLINDINGLY PALE SKIN, THE PILGRIMS WERE MISTAKEN FOR MEXICAN ILLEGALS AND TURNED AWAY BY AREA BORDER CONTROL AGENTS WHEN THEY ATTEMPTED TO MAKE CAPE COD THEIR NEW HOME.* ☜ With the island playground of the affluent off the list of possible settlement destinations, the *Mayflower* voyagers decided to continue their search for a friendlier, British-appreciating location. In November 1620 they stumbled upon Plymouth and set up shop. As the 102 settlers collectively broke out singing The Soup Dragons' version of "I'm Free," a star was born.

We Will, We Will Rock You

Nearly 400 years after the fact, the Plymouth Rock landing is often regarded as simply the rumored site of where the *Mayflower* and its Pilgrims came ashore in 1620. It really is a nice way to say that they probably didn't land their ship on the rock, but since the locals have built a museum and carved out a tourist trap around the legend, most of us just play along.

While making plans to build on the waterfront in 1741, a ninety-four–year-old town elder named Thomas Faunce, the town's records keeper since the beginning of time, identified the precise rock where his father had claimed the Pilgrims set foot. Legend has it the old man took a swig of whiskey from his flask, walked the area, spun around three times, and pointed to the nearest stone. The scientifically selected rock quickly became famous as townsfolk and tourists stormed the harbor where the rock is located to get their pictures taken with it.

Rock Star

Plymouth Rock has enjoyed quite a history since being identified as the rock where the Pilgrims first landed, or quite possibly misidentified as the rock where the Pilgrims first landed. In 1774, the good people of Plymouth decided to move the rock. Their clumsy effort resulted in the rock splitting in half like an amicable divorce, so they moved half of the historic stone into the town hall. ☞ *YEARS LATER, THE CLEVER PEOPLE OF Plymouth DECIDED TO BUILD A WHARF OVER THE BOTTOM HALF OF THE STONE, AND IN 1880 THE TOP HALF WAS REUNITED WITH THE BOTTOM HALF IN A CEREMONY THE TOWNSPEOPLE CALLED "THE 69."* ☜ With the ceremony over and the rock now in permanent foreplay, the state of Massachusetts has created its smallest state park, Pilgrim Memorial Park, for everyone's voyeuristic rock viewing pleasure.

1587

1619 1620

Lost Colony
of Roanoke

Slavery Comes
to America

The Pilgrims Land
on Plymouth Rock

1626

Purchase of Manhattan

I'm sorry for your loss,
how much for the dining room furniture?

Controversy, Controversy, Controversy

Nothing drives the American shopping psyche more than the words "clearance sale," "fire sale," "going out of business sale," and the vulture-like "I'm sorry for your loss, how much for the dining room furniture?" estate sale. ☞ *The record books are littered with great deals; however, the all-time greatest bargain in U.S. history took place in 1626.* ✑ The transaction in question involved the savvy Peter Minuit, a Dutch explorer. Minuit represented the Dutch West India Company and was charged with the nonviolent acquisition of the land in question. He entered into negotiations with the Canarsee Indian tribe, believing they were the rightful owners of the land. Unbeknownst to Minuit, Brooklyn's Canarsees had only *posed* as the rightful owners of the land, situated on modern-day Manhattan. Whether they held a grudge or were just creative, they cleverly sold the land from under

1626

Purchase of
Manhattan

1681

Pennsylvania
and the Quakers

13

the feet of the Wappani Indians. Minuit was so attracted by the bright lights and adult video stores of Time Square that he entered into negotiations with the Canarsees not really caring who the land actually belonged to.

Minuit the Realtor

Unlike his negotiating counterparts, whose authority to enter into a sales trans-action for the land was suspect at best, Minuit acted with the full authority of the Dutch West India Company. Minuit was asked to secure a section of land from the locals that was suitable for settlement. Through Minuit's artful and peaceful negotiations, he acquired the twelve-mile island now known as the world's financial epicenter. The purchase price for this global business cradle was 60 Dutch guilders, the equivalent of about $24, or the cost of a hand job performed by an undocumented alien or a half-decent vibrator.

Shortly after getting his feet wet with his Manhattan deal, Minuit led a group of men in acquiring what would become Staten Island. The deal-making Dutchman developed a reputation for sweetening the deal with beads, tools, firewater and the always-popular peyote.

Your Fifteen Minuits of Fame Are Up

Capitalizing on his notoriety for making the big deal, Minuit was preparing to launch a series of how to make millions in real estate infomercials when the boat he was on encountered a powerful Atlantic Hurricane killing the Dutch-man and his crew. ☞ *As the boat went down, Minuit was heard saying "Princess Christina don't care about blonde people." ☜* With his legacy intact, Minuit will always be remembered as the man who bought Manhattan for the price of a hand job.

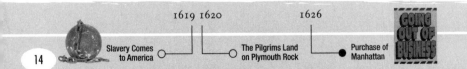

1681

PENNSYLVANIA AND THE QUAKERS

Simple, loose clothing is the trend that never ends

Friends with Tolerant Benefits

Tired of the religious intolerance that was practiced in dreary England, William Penn fled the land of royalty worshippers and pompous accents in search of a place with scores of tanned bodies and religious freedom.

Capitalizing on the growing demand for left-wing ideology, Penn used his father's circle of influence to orchestrate a land coup of what is now Pennsylvania and Delaware. Using the principles practiced in the Society of Friends religion, otherwise known as the Quakers, this area became known for its religious tolerance of anyone, regardless of whether they peed standing up or had a cup size of A through the gifted Pamela Anderson surgically enhanced model.

1681

Pennsylvania
and the Quakers

1692–1693

The Salem
Witch Trials

15

I Thought It Was Founded by Paterno

In England the Society of Friends was founded by an up-and-coming televangelist named George Fox. ☞ *Fox was popular with his followers even though he lacked the ability to heal the crippled and the blind with his own godly hands like America's millionaire TV preacher Benny Hinn.* ☜ In an effort to keep the operating costs of the start-up religion in check, Fox told his followers that God was found within each and every one of them, not the holy book. In addition to eliminating the need for Bibles, Fox also eliminated the need for churches. This savings in construction and building-maintenance costs allowed the Society of Friends religion to see earlier profitably and allowed them to quickly franchise into Pennsylvania with the help of Penn.

Once word of Penn's great experiment of religious tolerance, acceptance, and freedom hit the streets, thousands of non-Puritan, God-fearing, and sometimes Mohammed-loving fanatics uprooted their families and moved them to Pennsylvania, where they could openly express their religious freedom. Everyone from snake handlers to electricity-hating Mennonites began to practice their religion under the safety of Penn's umbrella of acceptance.

Group Hug

With love, peace, and happiness in ample supply, Penn extended his influence by setting up a democratic-style government that was designed to be hands-off. Quakers are known for their quirky ways of plain dress and rejection of material luxury. Simple, loose clothing is the trend that never ends. ☞ *They call it their "testimony of simplicity" while the rest of America calls it Hell.* ☜ In the end, if you are going to accept all people into a sexually repressed religious society, you will need some way to camouflage those who show up with Pamela Anderson sized tatas.

1620 — The Pilgrims Land on Plymouth Rock

1626 — Purchase of Manhattan

GOING OUT OF BUSINESS

1681 — Pennsylvania and the Quakers

THE SALEM WITCH TRIALS

. . . most often hanged, but sometimes burned at the stake to keep things fresh and interesting

Witchy Woman

All information from this point forward was conjured up with a Ouija board and chants of "light as a feather, stiff as a board." We were sitting in a dark room with lit candles, and as the scent of "ocean boardwalk" collided with "summer linen," a power from another world instructed us to write about the Salem Witch trials. Spooky, no?

Massachusetts has a lot to brag about when it comes to finding witches and people who don't root for the Red Sox. ☞ *BETWEEN THE YEARS 1692 AND 1693, MORE THAN 150 PEOPLE WERE ARRESTED IN THE NEW ENGLAND AREA FOR PRACTICING WITCHCRAFT AND POSSIBLY BEING YANKEE FANS.* ☜ The initial outbreak was in 1692 when a group of young girls called the "Circle Girls" got together to discuss icky boys and Pilgrim fashion trends.

One of the "Witchy" games they played was to crack an egg into a glass of water and see what shape it formed. One night, Ann Putnam, who was twelve, saw the shape of Hugh Heffner. Soon afterward Ann, Betty, Paris, and Abigail began acting like something out of *The Exorcist*. Today this would be recognized as behavior typical of preteens who didn't get an iPhone for their birthday. When their behavior caught the attention of the local Puritans, Ann was asked to name those who tormented her. She accused Martha Corey, a church member who wore her girdle tight and kept her morals even tighter. Despite there being no evidence of Martha's tormenting skills, she was successfully hanged. The people of the community began to freak out; irrational thinking spread everywhere, with concerns that any one of them could be a witch. As people were arrested, the execution orders were swiftly handed down. Those convicted of witchcraft charges were most often hanged, but sometimes burned at the stake to keep things fresh and interesting.

The Great Repression

The Puritans were boring and most certainly a little repressed. The Puritans believed that kissing with tongue involved witchcraft, meaning that any mouth to P action was punishable by, well, the same as witchcraft, only more public and painful in order to serve as a deterrent. Even music was considered evil, and funk music made the town elders explode. ☞ *Think **Footloose**, minus the colonial Kevin Bacon to show these people the way.* ☜ It was against the law not to attend church, and men and women sat separately so as not to distract each other, which happened often when the women wore their shoelace-high skirts.

1681

1692–1693

18   Pennsylvania
and the Quakers

The Salem
Witch Trials

As for the accusing-natured Ann, the accusations just kept rolling in. She ended up pointing the finger at sixty-two different people in all. Her parents, ever the pious Puritans, enjoyed the executions so much they got into the accusation game also. With so many people being sentenced to death, area residents could often be heard playing the "if given a choice, will you choose, boiling, hanging, burning, or quartering" game. ☞ *YEARS lATER, ANN cAME clEAN ANd told TMZ.com tHAt mANy of hER ACcUSAtioNS WERE fAlSE.* ▣

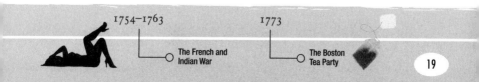

1754–1763

The French and
Indian War

1773

The Boston
Tea Party

19

THE FRENCH AND INDIAN WAR

The French teamed up with the Indians, promising silk scarves for everyone upon victory

Stranger Than Clooney-Rosie O'Donnell?

Remember the first time you watched porn? You were wondering why the short troll-like gentlemen got to "act" with the gorgeous blonde with the perfect larries. Then he got de-pantsed, and not only was the dude huge, he could also outlast you and three of your friends. The brilliant script had brought together a strange combination. If bagging a chick like that seems off the radar for most, an alliance between fiercely capable Indian warriors and a French military more interested in sharing a glass of Merlot than scalping their next victim was even stranger. It is this combination during the French and Indian War that tops the list of most unusual wartime playmates.

1692–1693

The Salem
Witch Trials

1754–1763

The French and
Indian War

Taking place on American soil from 1754 until 1763, the French and Indian War is a war known by many names. This enjoyable nine-year confrontation is also known as the Seven Years War in honor of the length of time from the official declaration of the war in 1756 to the treaty signing in 1763. In the land of impressionist painters, the French call it "Guerre de Sept Ans" which also translates to "seven years war," but when it is said in French it sounds like an effeminate growl.

Your Basic "Smash-and-Grab" Job

Unlike many of the more popular wars of today, this conflict was about land and not religion. ☞ *Realizing that the United States was an ideal location to expand cabaret dancing, the French sent their soldiers south down the Ohio River in the neighborhood of modern-day Pittsburgh.* ☜ They teamed up with the Indians against the British, promising silk scarves for everyone upon victory.

The fighting was fierce, as French soldiers nibbled exotic cheeses like gay mice and shooed the British out of the area. The French enjoyed important victories at Fort Oswego, Fort William Henry, Fort Duquesne, and Carillon. But, as quickly as a high school male getting laid for the first time can achieve liftoff, the tide turned and the British were celebrating their war effort with warm beer and fish and chips.

To the Victor Goes the Syrup

With the spirit of the French broken and the Indians wondering what could have been, the war officially ended on February 10, 1763, with the signing of the Treaty of Paris. This treaty stripped the French of all of their North

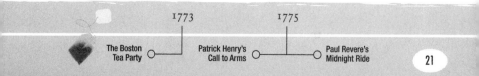

1773

1775

The Boston
Tea Party

Patrick Henry's
Call to Arms

Paul Revere's
Midnight Ride

21

American territory east of the Mississippi except for a couple of small islands off the coast of Newfoundland. In exchange, the French regained control of the Caribbean Islands of Guadeloupe and Martinique, which were being controlled by the British at the time. The Spanish found a way to get their hands on Louisiana for their loss of the sunshine state of Florida to the British. ☞ *And to the victor went the spoils, with the British receiving all of Canada and the unlimited supply of maple syrup that came with it.* ✍

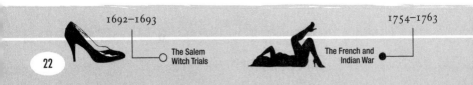

1692–1693
The Salem
Witch Trials

1754–1763
The French and
Indian War

1773

THE BOSTON TEA PARTY

An effort was made to turn away BEI's ships like same sex lovers at a Focus on the Family conference

A Quick Game of Monopoly

By 1773, the colonists had developed a "fuck you" attitude toward the mother country. Tired of the British attempts to control the settlers in the New World, many of the early arrivers to the area began looking for ways of establishing their own economic and social identity. For some of the newbies who packed their entrepreneurial spirit with them, it became a popular practice to smuggle tea into the colonies. Steve Jobs and Michael Dell wannabes like John Hancock could sell their circumventive tea at a lower price, as the legitimate British tea that was being imported had a colonial tax imposed on it by the British Parliament.

The powerful British East India Company was responsible for importing their tasty tea into the colonies. It appeared to the BEI that tea smuggling had taken on a hugely popular multilevel marketing platform, as their sales in the

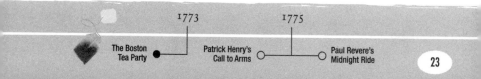

1773 1775

The Boston
Tea Party
Patrick Henry's
Call to Arms
Paul Revere's
Midnight Ride
23

colonies dropped from 320,000 pounds per annum to a mere 520 pounds per annum, or the approximate weight of Republican radio host and prescription drug enthusiast Rush Limbaugh's ego. Facing large debts and a huge supply of tea with nowhere to sell it as the colonial tax made it impossible to compete on price, the BEI begged for help from the British government.

In response to BEI's fit throwing, the British passed the "let's try and please everyone" Tea Act. This piece of legislation allowed the BEI to import their delicious tea into the colonies completely tax free. By removing the tax, BEI could now sell their tea for even less than those participating in Amway's smuggled tea pyramid. The king's representative in the colonies, Lord North, nicknamed Peter for the use of his outrageously long tea spout, figured it would be a winning deal for all involved. Instead, the settlers saw the removal of the tea tax as a way of creating an instant tea monopoly for BEI in the colonies.

Take This Tea and Shove it

The wig-wearing British Parliament underestimated the effects of the 1773 Tea Act coming on the heels of the 1767 Townshend Acts, which came on the heels of the 1765 Stamp Act. Many in the colonies were *steamed* about taxes being implemented and changed without having a say in the matter. ☞ *Out of frustration, the famous line "No taxation without representation" became popular as Amway salesman started selling hats, T-shirts, and bumper stickers to their family and friends with the slogan printed on it.* ☜

The appearance that the British government was attempting to create a monopoly on tea sales for the BEI Company was the final straw for many colonists. An effort was made to turn away BEI's ships like same sex lovers at a Focus on the Family conference before they could even make landfall. However, in Boston the BEI had the support of the pro-British governor, and they were able to make it into port with their cargo of tea.

1754–1763

The French and
Indian War

1773

The Boston
Tea Party

On December 16, 1773, the night before the tea was to be unloaded, approximately sixty local Boston residents, believed to be led by Samuel Adams, dressed up as Mohawk Indians and boarded the three ships, the *Dartmouth*, the *Eleanor*, and the *Beaver*, and began destroying the cargo. Nonparticipating witnesses have said the colonists dressed up not only as Indians, but also as police, construction workers, sailors, and cowboys, and that the after-party really got out of hand. Police reported hearing loud chants of "Y-M-C-A," but nobody seemed to understand its relevance. ☞ *Once the ships were boarded, they didn't bother to steal the tea, they simply dumped all 342 crates of tea into Boston Harbor while dancing to a funkadelic disco beat.* ☜

Party Like It's 1773

Reaction to this Tea Party was mixed at best. Colonists such as Ben Franklin were on record condemning the act, and Franklin even offered to pay the British back out of his own resources. The British were shocked, to say the least. Fashionistas were said to decry the costume choices by the colonists. The British were angry, and like a parent putting a young child in time-out, the British closed the port of Boston immediately and went on to pass the "Intolerable Acts." These acts were set in place to punish this kind of resistance in the future. They are also credited as being one of the events that led up to the Revolutionary War, which granted the colonists their independence from the British. Recently, it has been speculated that the British have sought revenge against the United States with attempts to make us watch Hugh Grant movies and soccer games. However, quick-thinking Americans have struck back by stealing many generations of English chefs and dentists, causing an epidemic in England of poor teeth and horrible food.

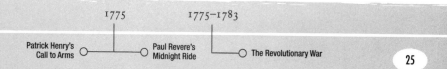

1775 — Patrick Henry's Call to Arms

1775 — Paul Revere's Midnight Ride

1775–1783 — The Revolutionary War

1775

PATRICK HENRY'S CALL TO ARMS

"Just Win, Baby"

High Maintenance

The Henrys were a demanding family. It was in their blood. John Henry demanded sex on a regular basis and his wife was happy to accommodate. The byproduct of their frequent encounters was eleven children, including the favored Patrick Henry. Known to have the characteristics of a Latin lover long before there were Latin men living the American dream, John proved to have the sexual stones and genetic make up to produce offspring with great oratory skills.

Demanding Education

As parents, John Henry and his wife Sarah Winston Syme were a demanding pair. They ordered their kids to eat their vegetables and were just as inflex-

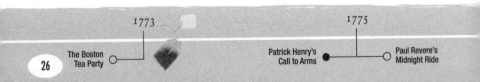

1773

The Boston
Tea Party

1775

Patrick Henry's
Call to Arms

Paul Revere's
Midnight Ride

ible when it came to education. *FEARING his inability to coordinate parent-teacher conferences for all eleven of his kids, John chose to educate his kids at home.* By home schooling Patrick and his siblings they were able to avoid all the hazards that children who attended traditional government-run schools in the 1700s were forced to deal with. The pressure to decide whether or not to join a gang, who to bring to the prom, or whether the blonde on the bus or the brunette in homeroom was most likely to put out were things the Henry children did not have to deal with. Released from these stresses, Patrick was free to learn the skills from his father that would eventually land him a wife with an attractive dowry.

Demanding Marital Bliss

Swearing off sex before marriage, Patrick used his father's virility as proof that the Henrys were accomplished sexual performers and that any woman who would commit herself to him would be in line for some off the charts satisfying encounters. Confident he was a solid catch, Patrick followed the Henry family tradition and demanded a dowry in return for giving his bachelorhood away.

The first to take the bait was Sarah Shelton, a horny Virginia girl. With her came a 600-acre tobacco farm and six slaves as a dowry. Unfortunately for Patrick, none of the slaves were of Native American heritage. This proved to be important when a severe drought hit Virginia and none of the African slaves working the land could muster up an adequate rain dance to bring much needed precipitation to the Henry farm. Upset with his slaves for not making it rain when they were told to, Patrick sold the six underperforming slaves to raise enough capital to start a store. Unfortunately, Patrick's father was an underwriter for Countrywide Home Loans, so when he taught Economics 101 to the Henry kids, he taught them to extend credit liberally.

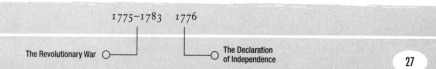

1775–1783   1776

The Revolutionary War ○——┘   └——○ The Declaration
                                                    of Independence

☞ Patrick's Freddy Mac-like lending practices resulted in the busi-ness failing ☜

The Most Famous Demand

With a failed farm and a failed business on his resume, Patrick relied on his father to call in a couple of favors from his friends of influence. With a little arm twisting Patrick was granted a license to practice law. Shortly thereafter, Patrick parlayed his newfound stature in the community into a seat in the House of Burgesses. Patrick used this platform to give one of the most famous speeches in American history. Using his enthusiastic hatred toward the British as a backdrop, Patrick spoke to the members of the House of Burgesses, and of course, made demands.

> *It is in vain, sir, to extenuate the matter. Gentlemen may cry, "Peace! Peace!"—but there is no peace. The war is actually begun! The next gale that sweeps down from the north will bring to our ears the clash of resounding arms! Our brethren are already in the field! Why stand we here idle? Is life so dear, or peace so sweet, as to be purchased at the price of chains and slavery? Forbid it, Almighty God! I know not what course others may take, but as for me, give me liberty or give me death!*

Although the last line was rich in hyperbole and lacked sincerity, Patrick's speech was well received by both the slave lords of the South and the carpet-baggers-to-be of the North, leading to an Al Davis–like, "Just Win, Baby" mentality that proved to unite and inspire those ready to resist the British. Henry's most famous demand became a rallying cry of sorts for colonists to throw off the British rule and to, of course, demand their freedom.

1773 — The Boston Tea Party

1775 — Patrick Henry's Call to Arms

PAUL REVERE'S MIDNIGHT RIDE

Let's have some porridge tomorrow morn. Shall I post thee or nudge thee?

Long Time

Paul Revere was a half-French colonist who at the time of his midnight run needed to get laid. He was in the midst of an all-time slump that he couldn't seem to break out of. No amount of clever pickup lines, begging, or alcohol seemed to get a woman of any race or attractiveness to open her pearly gates to him. He was at the receiving end of many jokes, mostly comparing him to a sexual camel that had a drink a long time ago and was now going through an obnoxiously long stretch without any action. ☞ *Within Paul's hometown he was quickly achieving the unwanted reputation of being a tad desperate, and even the stoutest of colonial ladies were turning him down on a regular basis.* ☜

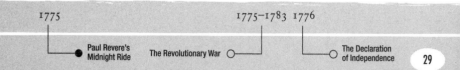

When Paul was asked to help the colonists cause by taking a midnight ride to warn of the impending British arrival, he was at first annoyed. He felt the main reason for the invitation was not his patriotism, bravery, or even his riding prowess; it was simply because everyone knew his late night calendar was painfully available. But as Paul began to sulk, he had the realization that going door to door warning of the British movement could actually prove to be a good way to meet ladies and end his own sexual problem of being "frequency-challenged," as he called it. He reasoned he could use the opportunity to fish with a much wider net and see who jumped in.

Slow Ride

The famous nighttime horse ride occurred over April 18 and 19 of 1775. Paul and a desperate but not *as* desperate fellow jockey, William Dawes, were instructed to warn John Hancock and Samuel Adams of the coming British troops. The nearly born again virgin duo took different routes to protect against both of them being captured at the same time. As they went through each town, they took the opportunity to knock on doors, asking to meet the lady of the house along with "Mind if I come in?"

Revere is known today for his midnight ride to warn citizens that the "British are coming!" All the confusion started when a poet named Longfellow immortalized Revere's ride in a poem. With a name like Longfellow, he was too busy shagging hippie chicks to fact-check. Historians continue to overlook that the real reason for the quest was to get laid. Thankfully at the next to last house Paul finally got invited in and four minutes later the quick triggered Revere changed his shouts from "the British are coming" to a more adult themed "Paul Revere is cumming! Paul Revere is cumming!"

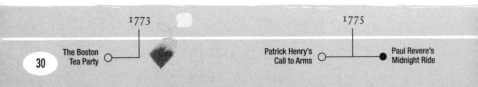

The Boston
Tea Party

1773

Patrick Henry's
Call to Arms

1775

Paul Revere's
Midnight Ride

A team of Cornell history majors have traced Paul Revere's sexual frequency issues back to his attempts to win female favor through his use of the following lame pick up lines.

- Let's have some porridge tomorrow morn. Shall I post thee or nudge thee?
- My love for you is like diarrhea; I simply cannot hold it in!
- Do you care for a raisin? How about a date?
- If I planted a garden, may I place our tulips together?

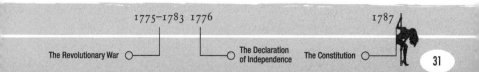

1775–1783 1776   1787

The Revolutionary War ○   The Declaration   The Constitution ○
                              of Independence

THE REVOLUTIONARY WAR

The teapot boiled over

Colonist Uprising

Colonists in the New World of America had become tired of the meddling and micromanagement of their affairs from the motherland of Great Britain. In 1775 the teapot boiled over, and enraged revolutionists stood up to the parent country and took control of the governments of the thirteen somewhat flourishing New World colonies. Not interested in family or small-group counseling, the revolutionists instead set up their own Continental army along with a Second Continental Congress to act as a quasi-national government in charge of the war effort to expel British troops from the newly named United States.

Patrick Henry's
Call to Arms

1775

Paul Revere's
Midnight Ride

The Revolutionary War

1775–1783

America's Army of Farmers

Months before the war with the British Empire commenced, the army ran endless print and television ads encouraging young males to be all they could be within the army of one. ☞ *The newly formed Continental Army offered $60,000 bonuses and chrome toasters for those willing to sign themselves or a family member up at www.goarmy.com.* ☜ Since the Revolutionary War preceded President Ronald Reagan's deficit defense spending model, the new recruits were asked to join other not so new recruits in bringing their sharpest knife to the fight, and keep to the "don't ask, don't tell" policy if they preferred fornicating with those of the same sex. Without government-issued uniforms the Southern soldiers were free to wear their favorite white wife beater shirts and the Northern combatants were okayed to wear comfort-fitting long johns of various colors. Since most of the soldiers were not career military-minded men, they often were forced to return home after a week or two of fighting the enemy, as they had farms to tend to.

Underequipped and underdressed for the occasion, the fighting farmers caught a break when they received legitimate war-winning weapons and stylish purple silk vests from the French government. ☞ *As a token of our appreciation, we sent the French former 21 Jump Street and Pirates of the Caribbean star Johnny Depp to Paris to live in return, knowing with his feminine mannerisms and quirky ways he would be a great asset to their society.* ☜

Five for Fighting

Geared up in his new silk attire, public servant and military enthusiast George Washington played the role of Commander in Chief of the fashionably

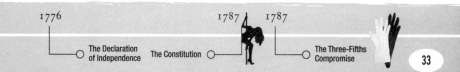

dressed ragtag army. As the fighting broke out, some colonies were valued more than others by England. Shaming the residents of the Keystone State forever, King George III was quoted in the *London Daily* newspaper saying, "It would be a joke to keep Pennsylvania" and quickly offered it back to the Indians in exchange for a series of commissioned totem poles depicting the hierarchy of the royal family. Once the totem poles were delivered to the British embassy in Washington, D.C., the mother country began losing interest in the war.

Following his shameful defeat at Yorktown in 1781, General Cornwallis threw in the towel like a good cut man should do. The Treaty of Paris was quickly written and signed off on allowing the British the opportunity to give up much of their land in America, for giving up the fight.

1775   1775–1783

Patrick Henry's
Call to Arms   Paul Revere's
                                Midnight Ride   The Revolutionary War

1776

THE DECLARATION OF INDEPENDENCE

Dragging on like a Keanu Reeves romantic comedy

Free-Range Americans

Since 1775, the Revolutionary War had been dragging on like a Keanu Reeves romantic comedy. Inside the thirteen colonies, farmers and more farmers were moonlighting as part-time militia combatants. The American army was short on military equipment but had a great supply of hoes.

Tired of the hours and the threat of death, a contingent of frustrated and unenthusiastic white military men convinced Continental Commander in Chief George Washington to allow black men to sign away the freedom that most of them did not enjoy and join white America's fight to free itself from the bonds of the even-paler-skinned British. As the war dragged on, with the assistance of new black soldiers, the great Caucasian minds of our founding fathers took to the less violent and subsequently less dangerous job of crafting a Declaration of Independence from the hygiene-challenged British.

The Most Famous Case of Plagiarism

As Congress met in June 1776, public support for independence was quickly swelling. This bulging of support was a reaction to King George's constant confrontational stroking of American tempers with unfair acts of taxation. With the chance for reconciliation now flaccid, America and its Congress took the bold step of approving a declaration of freedom and appointing a committee to draft such a document.

Thomas Jefferson, demonstrating that you need to work smarter and not harder, drafted the working copy of the Declaration of Independence between June 11 and June 28 in 1776. T.J. later admitted that the reason behind the quick turnaround of such an elaborate document is that he ripped most of it off from John Locke and the Continental philosophers. T.J. knew that if the United States did in fact win its freedom, copyright laws and enforcement were years away leaving him free to enjoy a Mötley Crüe–like harvest of adoring female fans attracted to his fame for authoring the most important document ever to be created in the United States. Locke, on the other hand, died in 1704 unknown and undersexed.

Maybe We Could Call It "Pre-Independence Day"

Jefferson wrote some of the first draft, plagiarized some of the first draft, wrote some more of the first draft, and plagiarized the rest before submitting the working document to the rest of the committee for their silent feedback. On the committee were recognizable names like John Adams and Ben Franklin, along with less recognizable names like Robert Livingston and Roger Sherman. ☞ *The families of Sherman and Livingston have taken out "Missing since 1776" billboards along most interstate highways since no one has heard from them since.* ☜

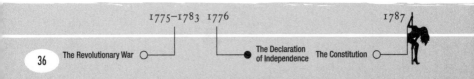

1775–1783 1776   1787

The Revolutionary War ○   The Declaration of Independence   The Constitution ○

With the committee's input mostly ignored, T.J. looked for a few more passages to borrow and then presented the final document to Congress on June 28, 1776. On July 2, 1776, with each colony receiving a single vote, the Congress adopted the document by a vote of twelve yeas and one abstention. The Congress had already voted thirteen "hell yeas" to zero "nays" in favor of wearing the funny white wigs. John Adams wrote to his wife that July 2 was destined to become a famous day in American history.

Surprisingly, Congress debated two more days on several sections, removing almost a quarter of T.J.'s originally crafted plagiarized document. ☞ *The most spirited debate between the North and South was the verse: "Slavery: Just say nay."* ✑ Ultimately, the verse was removed and an accord on the final wording for the declaration of Independence was reached on July 4, 1776. Abigail Adams, having jumped the gun with her entrepreneurial spirit, never did unload her "Peeing in British Tea since July 2, 1776" T-shirts and buttons.

1787

The Three-Fifths
Compromise

1789

George Washington Elected First
President of the United States

37

DECLARATION OF DEPENDENCE

As much as Americans value their independence, many famous stars find themselves dependent on their substance or compulsion of choice. See if you can match the star to their dependence:

1. Amy Winehouse

2. Robert Downey, Jr.

3. Charlie Sheen

4. Britney Spears

5. Eddie Vedder

6. Kurt Cobain

7. Courtney Love

8. Hugh Hefner

9. Oprah Winfrey

10. David Hasselhoff

11. Victoria Beckham

A. Prone to bouts of darkness and will assault you for singing his precious lyrics aloud without permission.

B. Twinkies, Twinkies, Twinkies!

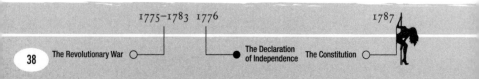

1775–1783   1776   1787

The Revolutionary War ○   The Declaration   The Constitution ○
                                              of Independence

C. Starred in an '80s flick where he had relations with men to pay for cocaine — we hope life never imitated art.

D. Dual addictions: looking cheesy and looking in the mirror at himself.

E. The second most addicted to sex on this list and that's amazing considering his track record.

F. Habitual flasher, never fails to participate in "No panties Thursday."

G. Sadly . . . heroin.

H. Outer addiction to women covers up his inner gayness.

I. One hot-selling record and a hotter-selling drug habit. Weekly interventions required.

J. Addicted to bad clothes, '80s sk8er hair, and frowning.

K. Public intoxication as well as drunk and disorderly beefs with the law.

Answers

1. I	7. K
2. C	8. H
3. E	9. B
4. F	10. D
5. A	11. J
6. G	

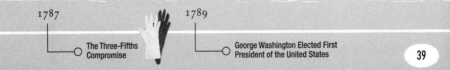

1787

The Three-Fifths Compromise

1789

George Washington Elected First President of the United States

THE CONSTITUTION

Much like a mafia family, it's only as strong as its weakest contributor

Three is the Magic Number

Whether you are studying ancient mythology or simply browsing in your local adult erotic store, you will occasionally encounter the vaunted beast of legend, the three-headed monster. The mythological sort is the chimera, a fierce creature with the heads of a snake, a goat, and a lion. If you happen to make a wrong turn, accidently get out of your car, trip, and fall into your local adult novelties shop, you may run into a totally different but equally scary three headed specimen. This monster has its own special purpose and its fierce heads can be made of sterile, semi-bendable plastic, or Pyrex. Debate rages on as to which of the two, three-headed monsters served as the inspiration for the three-headed model of government laid out by our forefathers in the constitution. ☞ *But much like the hair gel in Patrick Dempsey's medicine*

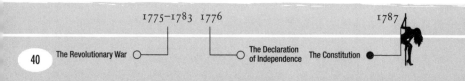

cabinet, the document gave our young but disheveled nation the shape and structure it needed to become great. 🔖

Lawful Head

The legislative head was the first one to bulge and strain the zipper of the constitutional pants. This particular part of the document entrusts the legislative branch with passing appropriate laws for the country to grow and prosper. The new proposed Constitution outlined a bicameral law-making branch consisting of a House of Representatives and a more respected Senate. The House of Representatives is based on unequal representation, meaning it matters how far sexually you would like to go with your prom date, but she still has the majority vote.

Conversely, the Senate is based on equal representation. One human year is equal to seven dog years and twenty-five guinea pig years. 🖙 *This type of structure ensures that all six residents of Montana can influence policy making while at the same time making sure California has a little more voting power, but not enough to force us all to drive a Prius while eating our alfalfa tofu guacamole wrap.* 🔖

Head Ruler

The executive head is the second part of the creepy three-headed monster. This section of the Constitution sets the ground rules for who can ascend to the lofty position of president of the United States. The most important part of this section is that it explicitly says that you must be a natural-born citizen and at least thirty-five years old to hold this office. This explains why motivated, hardworking baby Indians never get to serve in the role of commander in chief. It also explains why Arnold Schwarzenegger will never serve in the Oval

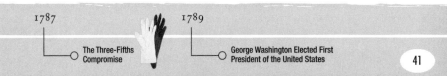

1787

The Three-Fifths
Compromise

1789

George Washington Elected First
President of the United States

41

Office. Even 220 years ago, the framers of the Constitution had the foresight to realize that only natural-born citizens are in tune enough with American's demands for outrageously high taxes, foreign energy dependence, high unemployment, and a semi-regular war to become the leader of this great nation.

Legal Head

Rounding out the trio of power is the judicial head. This partisan group is like our nation's *consigliere*, and is responsible for setting up the various levels of judicial interference and rulings. These lower courts are authorized to hear and adjudicate cases and hand down punishments. To ensure that the lower courts remain in check and follow the desires of the executive branch, a provision that allows the higher court to hear and overturn decisions was also included.

Amend This

Realizing the Constitution, much like a mafia family, is only as strong as its weakest contributor, otherwise known as Fredo, the framers wisely outlined procedures for amending the document to account for any treacherous Carlo Rizzi-like actions that went against the spirit of the document. ☞ *To date, Congress has been forced to pass twenty-seven amendments, including the President's right to keep a gun taped under the commode in the Oval Office bathroom in case of emergency or a surprise visit from a scary three-headed monster.* ☜

United States Constitution

Nothing gives you a sense of purpose in the morning like a quick read of the U.S. Constitution preamble. A fifty-one-word gem that helps you determine how your actions will best fit with the founding fathers' goals for the country.

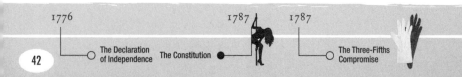

1776 — The Declaration of Independence   The Constitution ● 1787   1787 — The Three-Fifths Compromise

Please take a moment to read the nontruncated version of the Constitution preamble and then pause and a give some consideration to how your inspired choices for today will help America form a more perfect union.

We the people of the United States, in order to form a more perfect union, establish justice, insure domestic tranquility, provide for the common defense, promote the general welfare, and secure the blessings of liberty to ourselves and our posterity, do ordain and establish this Constitution for the United States of America.

If the above passage confuses you, don't worry—you are not alone. With the literacy rate of America well below the countries of Belarus and Tajikistan, you are simply a victim of a subpar education that was provided to you by the public school system before George W. rode into office with his cowboy hat on, declared that he loves children, even the difficult-to-teach ones, and that on his watch he wasn't leaving any child behind. If statewide standardized testing had been in place to ensure that the public schools you attended growing up were providing you with an above-Belarus education, you would understand what the founding fathers were striving for with the Constitution preamble and your role in accomplishing it.

The good news is that you are just one cog in the wheel of 330 million. This means that your contributions to the goals of the country are pretty insignificant. As a result, several occupations have written their own profession-specific preambles because it is much more likely that you can have an impact on the success of your employer than the success of the country.

Here is a sampling of how a handful of professions help to keep their workforce on track.

GARBAGE MEN

We the garbage men, in order to keep America clean, establish an orderly kitchen, and pick up, curbside, the crap you don't want, promise to do this to promote the general safety and welfare of America, and promise to do so for a minimum amount of money so as to not place an unfair burden upon Americans.

STRIPPERS

We the strippers of America, in order to keep stress on any male-female union, establish a penalty-free environment for men to treat us as objects and give a high-friction lap dance to help promote our own prosperity.

LAWYERS

We the lawyers, in order to form a less perfect union, promote our financial welfare above all else, and secure the blessings of wealth by charging obnoxious fees, do promise to slow down and complicate each and every transaction possible.

POLITICIANS

We the politicians, in order to form a more perfect union, establish justice, ensure domestic tranquility, provide for our re-election defense, promote the general welfare, and secure the blessings of lobbyists for ourselves and our posterity by taking bribes and/or campaign contributions, do hereby promise to spend every waking moment to make our Union perfect by assuring our re-election above all other goals and ideals.

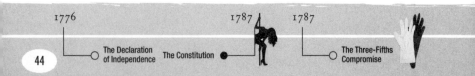

1776   1787   1787

The Declaration of Independence   The Constitution   The Three-Fifths Compromise

PROFESSIONAL ATHLETES

We the athletes, in order to form a more perfect sports world, establish wealth, ensure our own domestic tranquility, and provide for our sexual welfare, hereby promise to only have one girlfriend in each city, never take our wives on road trips, and strive to wear protection more than 50 percent of the time when having extramarital relations.

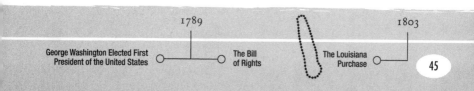

1789

1803

George Washington Elected First
President of the United States

The Bill
of Rights

The Louisiana
Purchase

1787

THE THREE-FIFTHS COMPROMISE

We bought 'em, we own 'em, we count 'em

Who's Bad?

The Philadelphia convention of 1787 set the stage for one of the great debates in American history. The two major questions that needed to be answered were whether or not before his death the King of Pop Michael Jackson had intentionally turned his skin pigmentation white in an effort to show his respect for the equally dead King of Rock 'n Roll Elvis Presley, and whether or not a person who has been purchased from a slave trader and given a lifetime of employment opportunity in one of the Southern states should be counted as a person.

Dirty Diana South

For Southern slave owners, the first question was easy. It was obvious that Michael's black to white transformation was the result of careful cosmetic en-

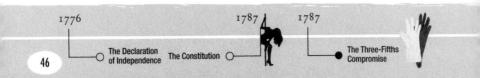

1776 — The Declaration of Independence   The Constitution   1787   1787 — The Three-Fifths Compromise

gineering motivated by his desire to thank Elvis for breaking down some of the racial biases that existed in the music industry before the draft dodging former Mississippian broke them down. The second question was a little more challenging. Slave owners all over the South were asking themselves, "If that slave I beat and whose wife I took home gains his freedom, what the hell will he do to me?"

It's Just the Way You Make Me Feel

For Northerners, Jackson's skin color getting whiter all the time had nothing to do with him being appreciative. It was clearly the result of a chronic auto-immune disorder called vitiligo where the body's own immune cells assault the skin's pigment resulting in a lighter more Justin Timberlake look. As for whether or not black people who were confined to a lifetime of servitude were in fact people, that was an easy one for Northerners. It was obvious that a slave was not a real person and should be counted as property not a person.

It Does Matter If You're Black or White

This divide in slave-counting philosophy became important in 1787 when the "we bought 'em, we own 'em, we count 'em" Southern states and the "we are above owning slaves" Northern states got together in Philadelphia to hammer out the makings of a Constitution. ☞ *After a few rounds of drinks at a local karaoke bar, it was agreed that Congress would be divided into two houses.* ☜ An upper house that called for equal representation for each state and a lower house that called for proportional representation for each state. As proportional representation was agreed to, it became necessary for each state's residents to be counted in order to determine how many congress-men would be eligible to represent their state in the lower house.

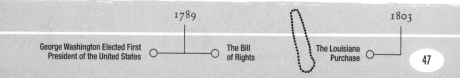

1789

George Washington Elected First
President of the United States

The Bill
of Rights

1803

The Louisiana
Purchase

47

The balance of power in Washington came down to the question how should slaves be counted? The slave-free states argued that only free citizens should count when determining representation. They knew that for years Southerners had become great customers of African slave brokers. And whether or not the slaves all looked the same, the Northerners knew there were tremendous numbers of them. If every slave was counted, it was obvious to the Northerners that the slave-loving South would run Washington.

Conversely, white Southerners knew how difficult it was to keep angry black men in line. They were not ready for this free-labor system to stop. ☞ *They were proud of their ability to grow their slave ownership despite the lack of tax benefits for doing so. They felt entitled to be rewarded for their hard work as slave owners.* ✐

With the Constitution hanging in the balance and the need for compromise more important than ever, the Northern states and Southern states agreed to a formula that would count each black slave as three-fifths of a person. It was reasoned that this would allow the Southern states to be compensated for their years of raising and training black slaves, but not to the point that it would be impossible for the Northern states to find equal representation in the new Congress.

As for Michael, the North and the South agreed to disagree on why he lightened up instead agreeing that ☞ *whether it was through cosmetic bleaching or vitiligo, the King of Pop died three-fifths black.* ✐

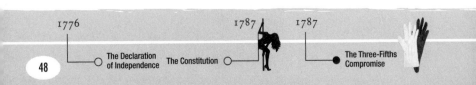

1776
1787
1787

The Declaration of Independence   The Constitution   The Three-Fifths Compromise

1789

GEORGE WASHINGTON ELECTED FIRST PRESIDENT OF THE UNITED STATES

The first in a near-perfect line of white presidents

A Cavalier Attitude

Benefiting from his parents' dislike for public education, George Washington enjoyed the rigors of his at-home-only education. Free from the restraints of an enormously underfunded public school system, young George took his home-schooled education with him when he joined the Virginia Militia days after hitting puberty, earning the distinction of lieutenant colonel at the MySpace-obsessed age of sixteen.

He Was Possibly Surveying Your Wife

In addition to being an enthusiastic killing machine, Washington moonlighted as a surveyor, measuring and plotting the earth's surface. He could tell you where your yard ends and your neighbor's yard begins, and whether it was okay

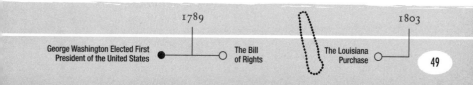

1789

1803

George Washington Elected First
President of the United States

The Bill
of Rights

The Louisiana
Purchase

49

to ignore the imaginary boundary of physical property and enjoy an affair with the wife next door.

☞ *Although it wasn't his neighbor's wife, George did enjoy some extracurricular sex and fruity drinks with big-haired Jersey girl Mary Gibbons.* ☜ Despite Gibbons's best effort to satisfy George's Ron Jeremy–like appetite for off-the-charts action, rumors quickly spread of George's illicit parties with slave girls at his Mount Vernon home. Washington capitalized on these rumors by garnering the support needed to be appointed adjunct general of the Virginia Militia in 1752.

French and Indian War Involvement: Ridding the Colonies of Frenchies

In 1753 George had the honor of delivering a message from the British to the French while holding wine tastings in the Ohio Valley: Get the fuck out. The French ignored Washington, and actually captured George in a skirmish at Fort Necessity. He was released, and later he returned with British General Braddock in 1755 to successfully kick the French out. Tired of a soldier's life, Washington turned his back on public service and retired to his Mount Vernon estate, where he satisfied his need for "strange" by marrying a serviceable widow named Martha Dandridge Custis. Following the honeymoon, George went into semiretirement for several years, farming and partying with the woman that he held the title to at his Mount Vernon home.

Next Up: Kicking the British Out

George took an active interest in the feud between the colonists and the British. As tensions escalated, George, ever the public servant, was sucked back into action. He left the cushy retired life and attended the meeting of the

Second Continental Congress in Philadelphia as a delegate from Virginia in 1775. There he was elected the commander in chief of the ragtag Continental army. After approximately six years of cat and mouse, the British tired, and Washington accepted British surrender from General Cornwallis at Yorktown in 1781. Washington re-retired, or so he thought, to Mount Vernon.

From Shuffleboard to the White House

After years of successful military leadership culminating in the surrender of the crotchety old General Cornwallis at Yorktown in 1781, Washington was enjoying a re-kindling of marital flames with Martha, however, his inability to walk away from the young nation's problems led him to the Constitutional Convention in Philadelphia in 1787 and ultimately back into service for his country. George benefited from the idea that letting every citizen have a voice in their leadership would be time consuming, expensive and, unnecessary. The Electoral College did away with the messy counting of Americans' votes, and in 1789, Washington became the first president of the United States as a handful of representatives forced their will on the rest of the country. George had the distinct honor of being the first of a near-perfect line of white presidents in American history.

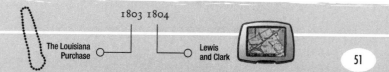

1803 1804

The Louisiana Purchase

Lewis and Clark

1789

THE BILL OF RIGHTS

Dirty little document

Not Just Another Bill

With the constitutional document already passed, James Madison began his Billy Graham–like crusade to protect the individual rights of priests, strippers, drug dealers, thieves, and the common man. He proposed twelve constitutional amendments (of which ten were passed) during a congressional all-night cocaine binge in New York City on September 25, 1789. With angel dust all over the historic manuscript, Bill O'Reilly of Fox News reported that the dirty little document was sure to be the most litigated legislation in American history. The signing of the Bill of Rights effectively provided for the following guarantees:

FIRST AMENDMENT. *Congress shall make no law respecting an establishment of religion, or prohibiting the free exercise thereof, or abridging*

the freedom of speech, or of the press; or the right of the people peaceably to assemble, and to petition the Government for a redress of grievances.

The first amendment protects crazy Pentecostal Church of God attendees, allowing them to handle deadly snakes and drink rattlesnake venom during service while at the same time allowing the *National Enquirer* to report on political commentator Dick Morris's fetish for sucking the toes of prostitutes.

SECOND AMENDMENT. *A well regulated militia, being necessary to the security of a free State, the right of the people to keep and bear Arms, shall not be infringed.*

This little beauty protects the rights of gangsters and rednecks to own truckloads of pistols, AK-47s, hand grenades, and atomic bombs.

THIRD AMENDMENT. *No Soldier shall, in time of peace, be quartered in any house, without the consent of the Owner, nor in time of war, but in a manner prescribed by law.*

This amendment prohibits the men serving in our military to sleep with another man's wife without his consent.

FOURTH AMENDMENT. *The right of the people to be secure in their persons, houses, papers and effects, against unreasonable searches and seizures, shall not be violated, and no warrants shall issue, but upon probable cause, supported by Oath or affirmation and particularly describing the place to be searched, and the persons or things to be seized.*

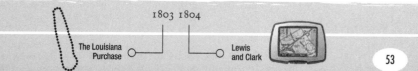

This amendment makes it much more difficult for police officers to search the trunk of Snoop Dogg's car just because he is black and looks high.

FIFTH AMENDMENT. *No person shall be held to answer for a capital, or otherwise infamous crime, unless on a presentment of indictment of a Grand Jury, except in cases arising in the land of naval forces, or in the Militia, when in actual service in time of War or public danger; nor shall any person be subject for the same offence to be twice put in jeopardy of life or limb; nor shall be compelled in any criminal case to be a witness against himself; nor be deprived of life, liberty, or property, without due process of law; nor shall private property be taken from public use, without just compensation.*

This amendment was written to ensure that O.J. Simpson never has to explain the cuts on his hands, the bloody Bruno Mali shoe prints, the missing clothes, and the loud sound outside Kato Kaelin's bedroom. It also makes sure that just because of the incompetence of District Attorney Marcia Clarke and her overwhelmed assistant district attorney Christopher Darden, O.J. cannot be tried again on the criminal charges of killing his ex-wife and her eyeglass-returning good Samaritan friend, Ron Goldman.

SIXTH AMENDMENT. *In all criminal prosecutions, the accused shall enjoy the right to a speedy and public trial, by an impartial jury of the State and district wherein the crime shall have been committed, which district shall have been previously ascertained by law, and to be informed of the nature and cause of the accusation; to be confronted with the witnesses against him; to have compulsory process for obtaining Witnesses in his favor, and to have the assistance to Counsel for his defence.*

1787
The Three-Fifths Compromise
George Washington Elected First President of the United States
1789
The Bill of Rights

This amendment ensures that not only are tax payers required to pay for the incarceration of the poor, but they are also required to pay for their subpar defense.

SEVENTH AMENDMENT. *In suits at common law, where the value in the controversy shall exceed twenty dollars, the right of trial by jury shall be preserved, and no fact tried by a jury shall be otherwise re-examined in any Court of the United States, than according to the rules of the common law.*

This allows endless lawsuits in federal court that require the use of a jury of your peers who were too dumb to avoid jury duty.

EIGHTH AMENDMENT. *Excessive bail shall not be required, nor excessive fines imposed, nor cruel or unusual punishments inflicted.*

Unfortunately, this has all but ended modern-day firing squads here in the United States.

NINTH AMENDMENT. *The enumeration of the Constitution of certain rights, shall not be construed to deny or disparage others retained by the people.*

This special clause allows for the fact that much of what needs to be protected has been left out of the Bill of Rights. This makes sure that whether it was intentional or careless, the citizens of the United States are not limited to the rights outlined in the Bill of Rights. This vague amendment makes room for women to choose contraception and abortion.

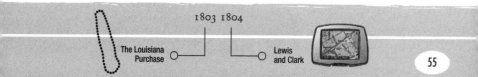

1803 1804

The Louisiana Purchase

Lewis and Clark

TENTH AMENDMENT. *The powers not delegated to the United States by the Constitution, nor prohibited by it to the States, are reserved to the States respectively, or to the people.*

This allows the federal government to defer back to the states any issues it finds too complicated or divisive to deal with on their own, like the legal age of sexual consent.

1787

1789

The Three-Fifths Compromise

George Washington Elected First President of the United States

The Bill of Rights

THE LOUISIANA PURCHASE

...forced to don a beret and pretend he appreciated the works of French impressionist painters

T.J. Loved the Magic Beads

President Thomas Jefferson, looking to expand the size of the United States, was hopeful that the Spanish government would agree to sell the Louisiana Territory to him for a price that even those enjoying the financial freedom of living below the poverty line could afford. Instead, Spain's King Charles IV turned over the territory to the French as an apology for a Spanish cycling team failing a post-race drug test in the Tour De France of 1802. Now that the territory was owned by the difficult-to-deal-with French, the United States lost the right to use the New Orleans port's warehouses to store the magical beads that encourage woman of various breast sizes to remove their tops for the viewing pleasure of an intoxicated male audience during Mardi Gras every year. Jefferson was now forced to don a beret and pretend he appreciated the

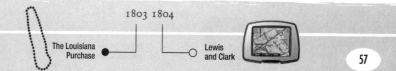

works of French impressionist painters in an effort to acquire the land he so dearly desired.

A "We're Going to War" Sale

Jefferson and his secretary of state, James (Dolly) Madison, began diplomatic efforts with the French in lieu of the more popular military option. In hopes of finding a John Lennon–inspired "give peace a chance" solution, Jefferson sent Madison to Paris as a diplomat. Upon Madison's arrival, he was pleasantly surprised to hear that Napoleon's desire to conquer Europe was suffering through a lack of funding and the French plan to re-establish itself in the United States was being abandoned. France's minister of finance advised the French government that they could not afford to send troops to occupy the entire Mississippi Valley. ☞ *He warned that if a conflict broke out, the hygienist-free British would come down and attack from John Candy's homeland, resulting in heavy losses both financially and militarily.* ☜ The minister viewed the area as a liability, apparently knowing nothing of the properties of the magical New Orleans beads. Fortunately enough, Napoleon's need for cash motivated him, and he agreed with his advisor, coming to the conclusion to sell the territory to the land-hungry United States.

Desperately needing cash, the French quickly agreed to sell the Louisiana territory including New Orleans for $15 million, an amount that far exceeded what Jefferson had authorized. The purchase effectively doubled the size of the United States, making room for illegal immigrants for centuries to come. The approximately 600 million acres were acquired for about four cents an acre or the equivalent of modern-day real estate values in Nebraska.

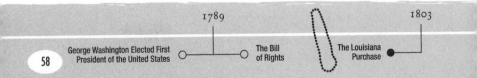

1789

George Washington Elected First President of the United States

The Bill of Rights

1803

The Louisiana Purchase

1804

LEWIS AND CLARK

Known as seasoned travelers, they always packed each other's stuff the night before a trip

Jefferson's Wet American Dream

President Thomas Jefferson found the distractions of running the day-to-day operations of the country annoying and time consuming. There never seemed to be enough Tom time. No time to sit down, relax, and just daydream anymore. In fact, the only time T.J. got for himself was the time spent on the presidential commode. While locked up in the latrine, he often dreamed of an expedition to the western portion of the continent. The land was undiscovered, and Jefferson hoped to find a path to the Orient to increase U.S. trade and import wild Asian strippers to help entertain donors for his re-election campaign ☞ *The only thing holding him back was his fear of a French guy with a little-man's complex, Napoleon Bonaparte.* ☜ Bonaparte and the French were holding claims on the land that stood between Jefferson and the discovery of the Northwest Passage. Never the bully and always the

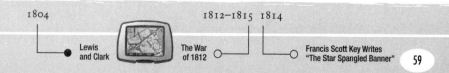

bullied, Jefferson was fearful of sending explorers into the western wilderness and stepping on Bonaparte's miniature French toes. Jefferson's fears were eased when Bonaparte offered to sell the 90,000 square miles west of the Mississippi River.

Jefferson jumped on the opportunity and sent Bonaparte $15 million to finance his continued destruction of Europe. In retrospect, many Americans feel we were screwed on the deal. The land purchased by T.J. became Arkansas (we could have done without), Iowa (definitely didn't need), Kansas (still don't need), Minnesota (see Iowa), Montana (a place for people who don't like people), Missouri (see Arkansas), Nebraska (nice addition—everyone likes corn), South Dakota (even the Indians won't take it back), and Wyoming (see Montana).

During his time in office, under the direction of White House senior advisor Karl Rove, President Bush approached the French government requesting a refund for Missouri and Minnesota. Rove promised Bush he could use the refund to buy two dozen Hell Fire missiles and a three pack of the 20,000-pound bunker buster bombs to inflict additional suffering on the people of Iraq. Predictably, Dick Cheney offered to run the purchase through Halliburton and keep the Democrats in the dark about George's new toys.

Building the Dream Team

With no shortage of qualified candidates and plenty of out-of-work explorers to choose from, T.J. did what any sitting president would do. He hired a crony. Landing the job of director of western expansion was Meriwether Lewis. Realizing the trip was no weekend getaway and would likely last years, Lewis knew that he had to find a co-captain who was willing to swear off sex for a considerable period of time.

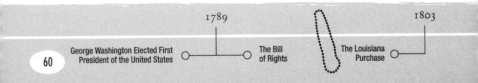

1789

George Washington Elected First President of the United States

The Bill of Rights

The Louisiana Purchase

1803

With no luck at the local seminary school, Lewis decided to ask born-again virgin and former military commander William Clark to be his co-captain. With the help of Lewis, Clark was able to assemble a cast of forty men who had more interest in rowing a canoe than getting laid to accompany them on their adventure out west.

☞ *HelP WANTed:*

AdVENTURERS WANTed! CAPAble outdoorsMEN Needed for EPic tRIP into the uNKNOWN. ReQuiRed skills iNCLude CARTogRAPHy, cooKiNG, wildlife taMING, NAViGAtioN, Ability to go long PERiods without food oR WATER, Ability to WALK for hours ANd/oR RuN for your life while cARRyiNG heAvy loAds of life-SUSTAiNiNG SUPPlies, ANd geNERAlly fENdiNG off deATh oN A dAily bAsis. No degREE ReQuiRed. ONly foRty Positions AvAil-Able, PleAse APPly iN PERSON. ✑

We'll Have a Gay Old Time

Known as seasoned travelers, Lewis and Clark always packed each other's stuff the night before a trip. And on May 14, 1804, Lewis, Clark, and approximately forty soon-to-be-sexually-suppressed men headed west.

As the adventurers moved on, and the long journey progressed, the team picked up some groupies, namely Toussaint Charbonneau and his fourteen-year-old Native American wife, Sacagawea. While most of today's fourteen-year-olds spend their time text messaging nude pictures of themselves, Sacagawea acted as guide and translator for Lewis and Clark, helping them trade with local Indian tribes for much-needed food. The frontiersmen quickly noted Charbonneau's young Indian bride, either with dismay or envy. ☞ *While being MoCKed About his wife's Miley CyRUS-like Age, ChARboNNEAU PROClAiMed thAt his Philosophy oN WoMEN WAS "go youNG oR go hoME."* ✑ After spending months on end with forty men in the wilderness, most of the

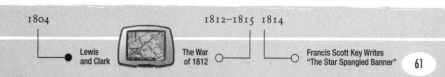

men wished Sacagawea had brought a sister along so they could stop contemplating trips to Brokeback Mountain.

The Motley Crew Comes Home (Sweet Home)

Lewis and Clark, their forty-man road crew, their Frenchman, and his underage wife finally made it to the Pacific Ocean in November 1805. Disappointed to learn that the banks of the Pacific Ocean were not fertile training grounds for strippers or Indian casinos, the dream team headed back east in March of 1806. Although presumed dead, the group returned after a long and grueling journey.

They were handsomely compensated for their efforts with both land and monetary rewards. While Clark went on to handle Indian affairs for the government out west, Lewis celebrated his accomplishments by committing suicide a few years later. Like most government projects, the expedition had gone past deadline and over budget. The original $2,500 budget came in at a cool $38,722, and Ben Bernake posted notices everywhere criticizing the government's lack of fiscal control.

Jefferson never got to live his dream of a trail to the Orient or the importation of lap dancers of any kind. Despite being unable to execute a simple re-election strategy from "Politics 101: Influence donors and key supporters with exotic strippers," Jefferson was still able to get re-elected and lead our nation for four more years.

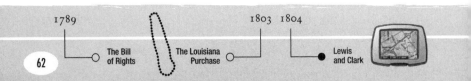

1789

1803 1804

The Bill of Rights

The Louisiana Purchase

Lewis and Clark

THE WAR OF 1812

Americans hated the British like Bill Clinton hates monogamy

Not Ready, but Willing

The war of 1812 started off with unprepared foes. Like a couple of horny teenagers fresh out of condoms, who have sworn off abstinence in favor of protected sex, the willingness was there but the preparation had been overlooked. Britain was a frequent war participator and found it hard to turn down any invitation to fight, regardless of distance or cause. At the time that they accepted America's invite for conflict in the United States, they already had their hands full with Napoleon's drive for total European domination. As for the home team, the American's were severely underfunded and underrepresented. Their navy was reminiscent of that of a 1600's landlocked third-world nation. ☞ *The term "ship" was used loosely, and the term "dingy" was generally more accurate.* ✍ But despite the lack of stockpiled resources on both sides, shots began firing and people started dying in August 1812.

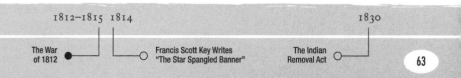

Coming off the heels of the Intolerable Acts, Americans hated the British like Bill Clinton hates monogamy. In an effort to eliminate the British from all of North America, the American military launched a series of wildly popular and unsuccessful attacks into the maple syrup–producing nation of Canada.

As retribution for American offensive efforts, the superior maritime vessels of the British formed a blockade around the U.S. coast, killing trade and sending the economy down like a $10 hooker. Despite their economic woes, the outgunned American forces continued to attempt to rid the continent of the pesky British and lay claim to their fair share of the sweet flavored pancake topper from Canada.

To the Victors Go the Status Quo

For the most part, the first couple of years of the war were uneventful for both sides. Both militaries enjoyed a series of back-and-forth victories and losses. Much of the landscape remained similar to what it was before the conflict began. For the monarch-worshipping British, the turning point came when Napoleon's European efforts were defeated. With the menacing Napoleon taken care of, the British were able to redistribute their armed forces and resources to the action here in the United States.

Reloaded with redeployed battle-tested veterans, the British met surprisingly little resistance as they marched single-file, wearing bright red vests, into Washington, D.C., where they burned the place down including President James Madison's love shack, otherwise known as the White House. After easily invading Washington, British commanders agreed to a plan of reacquisition.

Just as quickly as the tide had turned in favor of the Spice Girls' great-great-great-great-great-great-great-great-grandfathers, the U.S. military scored a game-changing victory when the U.S. Navy soundly won the battle of Lake Champlain, driving the British back into the frozen Canadian tundra.

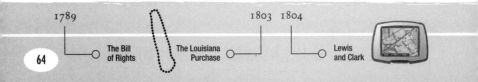

1789   1803   1804

The Bill of Rights   The Louisiana Purchase   Lewis and Clark

As word of the beat down reached the British team of negotiators responsible for agreeing to the terms of a peace treaty, the British quickly gave up their desire of laying claim to any U.S. territory and instead agreed to basically redraw the map of land ownership to its prewar positions. With the war over, American pride swelled like a college freshman, as the young nation had held its own against the evil British Empire.

Effectively, the War of 1812 concluded as a draw. Neither side had much to show for their efforts after the signing of the "lets make peace" treaty. But, with the battle-tested British fighting for their young Canadian brother, there was a lot of potential for this conflict to end in a Canadian land grab. For America, the battle of Lake Champlain was the difference maker. However, if the British/Canadian armed forces had proven victorious in this battle, it is likely they would have continued on their quest of acquiring more land in the United States.

In fact, it is possible that the entire contiguous land mass known as the United States would currently be flying the Canadian flag. The red, white, and blue would be the red and white. The army of one would literally be an army of one. Pictures of dead presidents on our currency would have to move over and make room for pictures of dead queens and equally dead prime ministers. ☞ *And most of all, there would be no second amendment debate, as the right to bear arms would be exchanged for the right to wear long underwear in the summer.* ☜

OH, CANADA

Since the United States was nearly Canada, the following multiple-choice, true/false quiz will test your Canadian IQ. Luckily, Canadians are known for being polite and forgiving, so you may take the test more than once and just like with the new SAT Score Choice, only your highest score will count.

Questions

1. Canadians abandoned the imperial measuring system years ago in favor of the more widely used international language of measurement the metric system. What is Canadian born actor Michael J. Fox's approximate height in centimeters?

   a. 57 cm.   c. 164 cm
   b. 245 cm   d. 327 cm

2. Approximately how many African-Canadians live in Canada?

   a. 600,000   c. 13
   b. 8,400,000   d. 3,500,000

3. Are American woman the only ones who marry older powerful and influential men?

   a. Yes   b. No

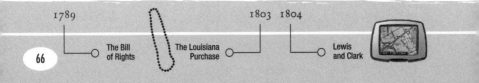

1789

The Bill of Rights

1803   1804

The Louisiana Purchase

Lewis and Clark

4. Canadians measure their outside temperature in degrees of Celsius not Fahrenheit. What is the equivalent U.S. measurement for 22 degrees Celsius?

    a. 57   c. 77

    b. 67   d. 87

5. Canadians are known for their love of beer; what is the most popular Canadian-owned brewing company in Canada?

    a. Labatt's Brewing Company Ltd.   c. Sleeman's Breweries Ltd.

    b. Molson Coors Brewing Company   d. Moosehead Breweries Limited

6. Which of the following porn stars was born in Canada?

    a. Tiffany Towers   c. Amanda Lexx

    b. Sunrise Adams   d. Sunny Lane

7. By government decree, what is Canada's national sport?

    a. Badminton   c. Hockey

    b. Lacrosse   d. Volleyball

8. True or False: Canadians have more annual sex than their American counterparts.

9. If you step on a Canadian's foot while waiting in line, should you:

    a. Apologize immediately   c. Pretend you rolled your ankle to gain the sympathy of your Canadian victim

    b. Ignore it and pretend like nothing happened   d. Wait for them to say they're "soorry"

10. True or False: Famed American talk show host Larry King has married Canadian before.

11. If the United States had become part of Canada, 99 percent of Americans (regardless of gender) would be playing hockey right now. True or False: Hockey skates are sized the same as shoes.

12. True or False: Canadian teenage girls are less likely to become pregnant than American teenage girls.

13. The country most similar to Canada in terms of population is:

    a. Afghanistan   c. Cambodia

    b. United Kingdom   d. Pakistan

Answers

1. **B.** Michael J. Fox, the popular star of the hit situational comedies *Family Ties* and *Spin City*, measures in at a less than average 5' 4½".

2. **C.** Currently, the Archers of Woodstock, Ontario, is the only black family living in Canada.

3. **B.** Although scores of American woman marry older influential men, Canadian-born Grammy award-winning artist Céline Dion proved that even Canadians are willing to sell their marital pride for their own economic benefit when she wed her manager, who happens to be twenty-six years her senior.

4. **C.** Only in America would meteorologists say the outside temperature will be a high of 77 degrees today.

5. **D.** It is a real hit to the Canadian ego but their most identifiable beers are now owned by foreign companies. Labatt's Brewing Company, Ltd. is now owned by the Belgian brewer Interbrew. Molson Coors Brewing Company is now less Canadian and more American. Sleeman's Breweries, Ltd. is now owned by Japanese beer makers Sapporo Breweries. This leaves Moosehead Breweries Limited as Canada's largest Canadian-owned brewery.

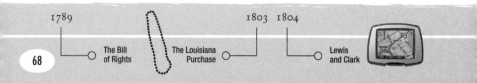

1789

The Bill of Rights

The Louisiana Purchase

1803 1804

Lewis and Clark

6. **A.** Tiffany Towers was born in Toronto, Ontario, in 1971, making her surgically enhanced 70FFF breasts ancient by the porn industry's standards.

7. **B.** Unofficially it might be hockey, however, in an effort to keep peace with the Indian population the government agreed to keep lacrosse as the official sport of Canada, recognizing its Native Canadian heritage.

8. **False.** The statistics don't lie. Americans have more sex. On average, Americans have sex 138 times a year, compared to the 105 times Canadians get busy annually. It is believed that the real reason for the disparity is the promiscuous nature of American high schoolers.

9. **D.** No doubt about it. Almost instinctively, a Canadian will apologize for getting in your way.

10. **False.** King is afraid that once he went Canadian he would never go back, and as he enjoys getting married often, he does not want to limited his applicant pool.

11. **False.** Depending upon the manufacture of the skate, most hockey skates run at least a size to a size and a half smaller than your shoe size.

12. **True.** On average, the Canadian teen pregnancy rate is significantly less than that of Americans.

13. **A.** Canada's human population is 33,487,208 and Afghanistan's is 33,600,937. If you marked "b" you are wrong, as the population of the United Kingdom is 61,113,937. If you marked "c" you are about equally wrong, as the Cambodian population is 14,494,293. And for those who marked "d," you are real wrong, as the population of Pakistan is a staggering 176,242,949.

After you have graded your test please proceed to the chart on the following page to determine your readiness to be Canadian.

1812–1815   1814   1830

The War
of 1812

Francis Scott Key Writes
"The Star Spangled Banner"

The Indian
Removal Act

0–3 correct answers: Yikes! You are not ready to eat gravy with your fries. However, you will now recognize July 1 as your new Independence Day.

4–8 correct answers: Nice effort. You can order Canadian bacon at a restaurant and your Thanksgiving is now celebrated in October and has nothing to do with the pilgrims.

9–13 correct answers: Outstanding. It is time to work on your Canadian accent to ease your assimilation into the Canadian culture. Hockey Night in Canada is now mandatory television viewing during hockey season. You understand that "God" can mean either God from heaven God, or Wayne Gretzky. Christmas is now a two-day holiday, as you will begin enjoying Boxing Day.

Regardless of your score, you must now end most sentences with the word "eh." It might seem awkward at first, but with enough practice it will become more natural. For those who struggle, it is suggested you practice in front of a mirror.

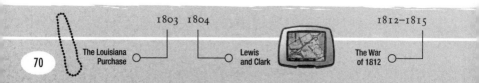

1803   1804

The Louisiana
Purchase

Lewis
and Clark

1812–1815

The War
of 1812

FRANCIS SCOTT KEY WRITES "THE STAR-SPANGLED BANNER"

Key's request to lay an urban beat underneath his poem was emphatically denied

F.S.K. the Attorney

Before guys like Francis Ford Coppola and James Earl Jones discovered that women love a man who is cool enough to use his whole name, there was a thirty-five-year-old hotshot named Francis Scott Key who had figured it all out.

Key was a successful lawyer who had made several arguments in front of the right-leaning advocacy group known as the United States Supreme Court. He was a perfect wingman at a bar and just the kind of guy you look for when one of your buddies gets picked up as a civilian by the British military and consequently made a prisoner of war. Dr. William Beanes was that buddy who was inconveniently taken into British custody after General Ross of Britain finished burning down nearly every political building in Washington including former President Bill Clinton's and Jenny Craig spokeswoman Monica Lewinsky's favorite White House venue, the oral office.

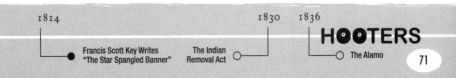

1814

1830   1836

HOOTERS

Francis Scott Key Writes
"The Star Spangled Banner"

The Indian
Removal Act

The Alamo

71

As Ross and his men were heading toward Baltimore harbor to catch a Ravens game and inflict additional casualties on the U.S. armed forces, Beanes's friends had FREE BEANES T-shirts designed and printed and then pooled some cash together to hire Key to seek his release with the help of Colonel John Skinner, the U.S. prisoner of war exchange agent. Shortly after Beanes's friends' retainer check cleared, Key found himself on a truce ship with Skinner, attempting to secure Beanes's release. After the successful negotiation, the three American amigos were detained on the ship, anchored eight miles from land, until the British attack was over. It was on this ship that Key the attorney became Key the poet, as he was inspired to write the words for what is now our national anthem.

Slap the Flag and Ride the Wave In

Four hundred five dollars and ninety cents went a long way in inspiring Key to write our sports pregame anthem. In the summer of 1813, major George Armistead, commander of Fort McHenry, wanted a flag so large that not only could a well-fed Kirstie Alley wrap herself in it but also any British naval ship could not miss his position. Mary Pickersgill, seamstress for hire, was contracted to make a 30' × 42' flag. For her efforts, she was paid the tidy sum of $405.90.

In addition to making the huge garrison flag, Pickersgill also made a smaller yet still plus-sized 17' × 25' storm flag for $168.54 to be flown during inclement weather. Key was able to draw much of his inspiration for the writing of our national anthem from the construction of the massive flag.

Gave Proof Thro' the Night

With Key and the other two non-Mexican amigos sitting on the truce ship outside the harbor, the British began bombing Fort McHenry at 6:30 A.M. on

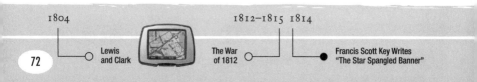

1804

Lewis
and Clark

1812–1815 1814

The War
of 1812

Francis Scott Key Writes
"The Star Spangled Banner"

September 13, 1814. Over the next twenty-five hours, the British pounded Fort McHenry like Jenna Jameson with heavy artillery and Congrove rockets. Key referenced the Congrove rockets' red glare in the sky with the line "and the rockets' red glare." Armistead had been flying the smaller flag throughout the rainy night of September 13, 1814. But on the morning of September 14, 1814, after Armistead and his men had taken the best the British had to offer, he ordered the larger garrison flag raised in an act symbolic of pointing an American middle finger at the British. It was on that morning after the brutal assault by the British on Fort McHenry that the $405.90 garrison flag inspired Key to write a poem about what he had witnessed over the preceding twenty-five hours.

The Poem That Became Our Anthem

Witnessing that the flag was still there after the British version of shock and awe tapered off, Key was so orgasmically excited that Fort McHenry did not fall into the hands of the British he began to write a poem with the dry and unpoetic title of "The Defense of Fort McHenry" on the back of a letter he was carrying. ☞ *The poem was four stanzas long; however, it is only the first stanza that was worth the scrap paper it was written on, and it has come to be recognized as our national anthem.* ☜

Since peace with the black man was even further removed than peace with the British, Key's request to lay an urban beat underneath his poem was emphatically denied by the hip-hop community of 1814. Instead, his words were later placed to the tune of a British bar song titled "To Anacreon in Heaven." It quickly gained Obamamania-like popularity, and the name was changed to "The Star-Spangled Banner." This catchy tune officially became our national anthem in 1931, when President Herbert Hoover signed a bill into law making "The Star-Spangled Banner" our official Olympic gold medal podium song of choice.

1830 — The Indian Removal Act

1836 — The Alamo

HOOTERS

1846–1848 — The Mexican War

1830

INDIAN REMOVAL ACT

Ability to bring a gun to a tomahawk fight was not impressive

This Land Is Your Land

After months of strategizing with key political confidants, tarot card readers, and a talented but unemployed horse whisperer named Shh-neigh-neigh, President Andrew Jackson, friend of the white man, orchestrated a plan.

His plan of presidential influence would earn him the love and adoration of screaming teenage Caucasian girls who were fearful of men with names like Bull Head, Catch the Bear, and Red Tomahawk. Jackson had long recognized that Euro transplants and their offspring deserved something special for making the long and difficult journey from the other side of the pond. They deserved what was already someone else's. They deserved to own the land that was inconveniently titled to men and women who were unaffectionately known as Indians.

These Indians had proven to be quite a pain in the ass when it came to providing the round football loving new arrivals with the means to make their economic dreams come true. In 1830, at a nationally televised debate against Chief Squatting Bull, Jackson effectively argued outside a popular Manhattan delicatessen that the United States could not be the land of opportunity if it didn't have any land to give away. ☞ *This argument inspired the white television audience watching at home like a David Hasselhoff concert inspires German freedom fighters.* ☜

This Land Is My Land

Prior to impressing debate monitors Wolf Blitzer and Anderson Cooper, hosts of *Squaw Box*, with his oratory skills versus Chief Squatting Bull, Jackson was winning millions upon millions of acres of Indian land as a respected military leader a decade and a half earlier. Those critical of Jackson's Indian bullying argued that his ability to bring a gun to a tomahawk fight was not impressive. Jackson's success over the Indians allowed white-skins in the South to start job programs for captured black Africans. The same black Africans whose egos were fed by the fact that white Americans cared enough to purchase them and provide them and their descendents with lifetime job security.

Riding the wave of enthusiasm from land hungry whites, Jackson ushered legislation through both the House and the Senate that gave him the authority to trade unsettled, undeveloped, and difficult-to-farm land west of the Mississippi River for the lush, developed, and agricultural friendly land owned by Indians east of the Mississippi River. Using the same algorithm that China uses to ensure that trade with the United States is not fair and equitable, Jackson began negotiating with the major Indian tribes to trade his desert for their arable farmland. Despite Jackson's one-sided good faith negotiations

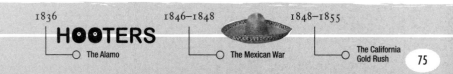

1836   1846–1848   1848–1855

HOOTERS

○ The Alamo   ○ The Mexican War   The California Gold Rush

with America's original settlers, many of them showed a total lack of appreciation for Jackson's land swap and refused to move.

Please Relocate in an Orderly Fashion

Despite Jackson's willingness to include colored beads in his crafty negotiations, there were some tribes who refused to play ball. This defiance left Jackson with no choice but to order General Petraeus to forcibly remove every Indian living east of the Mississippi. After years of indifferent results, the savvy Petraeus ordered a surge of military fighters. This surge in troop numbers proved to be the difference, as white America was able to rid itself of its pesky Indian problem and acquire the land they so richly deserved.

1812–1815   1814   1830

The War
of 1812   Francis Scott Key Writes   The Indian
                           "The Star Spangled Banner"   Removal Act

1836

THE ALAMO

Back like Montezuma's revenge

In Remembrance of . . .

Americans are lucky in that our country has a rich tradition of inspiring historically accurate stories to swell our pride to John Holmes proportions. Countries like Burkina Faso, Mauritius, and Kiribati exist in an environment void of any real significant reason to inspire national pride. Here in the United States, a young and attractive woman can truly achieve the American Dream by starting with nothing and achieving success. Starting as a Hooters waitress, wearing a tight-fitting tank top with skin-tight orange nylon shorts, to a shirt-removing, lap-dancing stripper, to a well-compensated international porn star, no mountain is too high. As for Kiribati, the women can't even find a Hooters, or even the poor man's equivalent, Wing House, to ignite their own inspiring tale. From U.S.-born-and-bred porn stars to gold medal Olympic efforts to military heroics on the battlefield, there are more chest pounding American

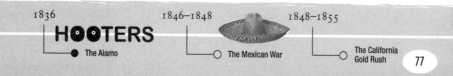

1836

HOOTERS
● The Alamo

1846–1848
○ The Mexican War

1848–1855
○ The California Gold Rush

77

events than we can ever be expected to remember. However, since 1836, we have been asked to remember to wrap it up when having sex with an evolved former Hooter's waitress and to remember the Alamo.

When it comes to Hooters girls it is best to form good habits. Wrap it up early and often. Get in a condom-wearing routine until it becomes second nature for you. As far as remembering the Alamo, dial back a hundred and seventy years or so as even back then thousands of unruly Mexicans were causing problems in Willie Nelson's home state of Texas.

The Battle Royal

In December 1835, Ben Milam led Texan troops against Mexican combatants stationed at the former home for missionaries and their converts known as the Alamo. After several days of intense fighting, the Texans were victorious. However, by February 1836, the Mexicans were back like Montezuma's revenge. General Antonio Lopez de Santa Anna brought his alternative late army to San Antonio, ready to attack.

Early on, the Texans made a unanimous decision (including the handful of nonvoting black slaves that were at the Alamo) that they were not going to surrender to a general with a girl's name. William B. Travis, mediocre warrior, but great community organizer, sent couriers out to ask for help, and with the few men who enthusiastically returned, the defense total reached approximately 200 versus around 8,000 Mexican troops.

Legend has it the motivational Colonel Travis drew a line in the sand and said all who wanted to stay and fight with him should cross it, and if there were any yellow-bellied sellouts, they were free to leave. Of course, the only one who did not cross the line was Moses Rose, who, naturally, was French.

☞ *His legend quickly became the yellow rose of Texas, or just "chicken shit" for short.* ✑

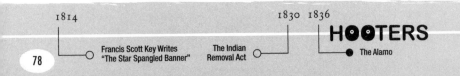

1814

Francis Scott Key Writes
"The Star Spangled Banner"

The Indian
Removal Act

1830   1836

HOOTERS
● The Alamo

Once the Alamo fell into Mexican hands, the final death toll was estimated at 189 Texan defenders, at least 1,600 Mexicans, and 208 Chihuahuas. Unable to find a battle in which 95 percent of their combatants died, in order to instill some reason for national pride, the governments of both Burkina Faso and Mauritius have applied for Hooters franchises to be built in their humble countries.

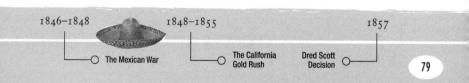

1846–1848   1848–1855   1857

—○ The Mexican War   —○ The California   Dred Scott ○—
                                Gold Rush   Decision

THE MEXICAN WAR

Without a Republican-inspired fence to keep them out

American Invasion

As José sipped away on his sweet tea he turned to look at the tavern door. "Oh, it's them again," he mumbled as the dirty Americans made their way into the bar. He didn't really like the Americans. Oh, they kept the neighbor's yard well landscaped and they were able painters, but they stilled annoyed José. They were probably here in the great territory of Texas illegally, he thought. José's government had encouraged some of these Americans to come in and make themselves at home, but this was getting out of control.

Such was the scene in the 1830s in the Mexican-owned territory of Texas. Mexico had secured the territory in a fistfight-with-guns military squabble with Spain in 1821. As part of the "we are now going to get along" peace treaty, they acquired the territories of California, New Mexico, and Texas. Following the conflict with Spain, the Mexican government was poor. Being unable

to rub a couple of pesos together for good luck, the government of Mexico encouraged American settlers to inhabit the area of Texas in hopes the Americans would bring their God-given guns with them to help protect the newly acquired land.

Without real border control or a Republican-inspired fence to keep them out, many more Americans settled in Texas than the Mexicans anticipated or wanted. The higher concentration of Americans, the natives' displeasure with the financial state of the Mexican government, and the lack of suitable drinking water caused the Texans to revolt in 1836, striving to gain their independence from the troubled poncho-appreciating nation of Mexico. When the revolution was crushed, the revolutionaries made overtures to the United States to annex their territory.

Mexican Buffet

As José rode his burro through town, he saw more Americans. Why did they have to come here? Of course sales of energy drinks and taquitos were way up, and if you needed a truckload of them, they were always available as day laborers, but the Americans were lazy and never showed up for work before 10:00 A.M.

Leading up to the Mexican war, the pacifist nation of the United States attempted to kindly purchase a large portion of Mexico's territory. But, despite their financial hardship, the Mexican government was confrontationally refusing to sell, obligating the United States to take it forcefully for the betterment of God's favored Americans. The conflict lasted from 1846 until 1848, with the United States emerging victorious.

War correspondents from Reuters were embarrassed by what they felt was a naked land grab by a stronger nation. The United States easily added the land that became the states of California, Nevada, and Utah. Not quite satisfied, they went back to the all-you-can-take land buffet and got seconds in the

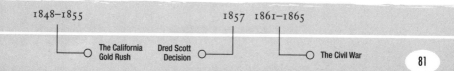

form of parts of Colorado, Arizona, New Mexico, and Wyoming. In an effort to show that the United States was fair and just, they wired $18 million dollars to the struggling Mexican government, which was about half what they had originally offered before they were forced into war by the unappreciative Mexicans.

As José arrived home, he passed yet another American restaurant that had sprung up in the area. Burritos and refried beans, yee-haw! All of their food tasted the same, and it was funny how they seemed to all have the same menu items numbered exactly the same way. No matter where you went, a number four was always two tacos (one chicken, one beef) with a side of rice and beans. José just hoped the government was going to do something to shore up the borders, as these Americans were taking over.

1830   1836   1846–1848

HOOTERS

The Indian Removal Act   The Alamo   The Mexican War

THE CALIFORNIA GOLD RUSH

Today, the American Dream consists of waking up with Paris and Britney.

Head West Young Man

The California gold rush was a period of time where anyone with a little determination and luck could achieve the American Dream. Today, with the Chinese and the European Union running our economy, the American Dream consists of waking up naked in a bed with Paris and Britney.

It was in 1848 that James Marshall discovered the precious metal in Coloma, California, that resulted in lottery-like riches for so many dreamers. ☞ *As rumors of the discovery spread like news of another Palin family teen pregnancy, many remained skeptical.* ☜ That is, until President James K. Polk confirmed the rumors on Hannity's America in December 1848, setting off a traffic jam on dirt roads headed west. As word spread of the many fortunes being made, people from all over the world flocked to California hoping to strike it rich. The pull of the gold rush was so strong it attracted

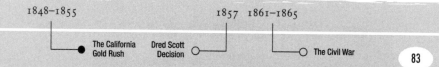

fortune seekers from Europe, South America, Asia, and even Australia. The land wasn't owned by any particular person or government at the time, so any gold you found was yours to keep. The first wave of dreamers were called "49ers" for the year they headed west. This massive quest for bling brought Hannah Montana–size crowds, as approximately 300,000 were reported to make the journey to the west coast.

San Francisco was a virtually unknown town when all of this began. In the first two years alone, its population grew from around 1,000 souls to an estimated 25,000 heartless gold diggers. For some, the attraction was gold, for others it was the city's tolerance for man-on-man action. Smart entrepreneurs opened up businesses around the boom. Mining-supply stores, saloons, hotels, restaurants, whorehouses, and gambling halls all showed up, as every vice was equally represented.

This massive influx of people led to the creation of here-today-gone-tomorrow mining towns. With all of the settlements and mining came disputes and the eventual creation of a set of rules to govern the area now known as California. In 1850, with all of its growth, California was admitted as the thirty-first state. Free from the class structure that was in place on the east coast, these trailblazers acted like Panama City spring breakers on steroids. Along with this freedom, wealth, and underdeveloped government came opportunity.

What Happens Here, Stays Here

As the rush continued, the gold began to disappear. As the gold dried up, miners continued to dream, working longer hours, filthy and unshowered for weeks at a time, taking on a resemblance to Jack Black. With the gold slowly disappearing from the area, hopeful miners turned to gambling, and if desperate enough, crime to help get by. It became harder and harder to find the golden shower they so desperately wanted. But the few who did hit the mother

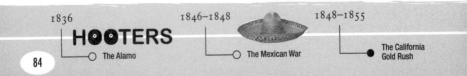

1836
HOOTERS
The Alamo

1846–1848
The Mexican War

1848–1855
The California
Gold Rush

lode even into the 1850s kept the hopefuls arriving. This environment of a very few well-publicized lucky winners among a sea of losers became the basic business model for modern-day Las Vegas. ☞ *This holds true for all Vegas casinos except for Caesars' Palace, where, when the Pussycat Dolls arrive, everyone wins.* ◁

Keep Dreaming

Up until this time in American history, the American Dream was of hard work, slow and steady results, building savings, and growing your wealth to join the growing upper-middle class. The gold rush of the 1850s changed all of that. Historian H. W. Brands noted, "The new dream was the dream of instant wealth, won in a twinkling by audacity and good luck. [This] golden dream . . . became a prominent part of the American psyche only after [Sutter's Mill]." Other than the holy grail of a Paris-Britney threesome, today, the American Dream for many has been reduced to hitting the jackpot on a scratch-off lottery ticket while chugging malt liquor in the gas station parking lot.

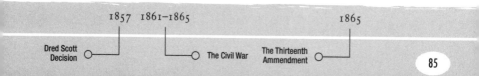

1857   1861–1865   1865

Dred Scott
Decision   The Civil War   The Thirteenth
                                Ammendment

DRED SCOTT DECISION

A financial no-brainer for white families that wanted to live a little bit of the good life

Slave Labor for the Benefit of All Non-Slaves

On March 4, 1857, as the new president, James Buchanan, took office, the issue of slavery was looming large across the United States. For decades, the fiscally irresponsible Northern states resisted slavery under the guise of human rights. Their argument was that their God was a loving God who created everyone equally. To the sadness of their bank accounts and shopaholic wives, they ignored the significant economic benefits that were associated with owning slaves.

The economic benefit to owning slaves was never-ending, including amortizing the initial slave purchase over the course of several years to lower your taxes. Besides, using proven "encouragement techniques," a slave owner could have their whole farm ploughed and replanted for what it costs the Chinese to make a cast-iron matchbox car covered in lead paint. Slavery was a financial

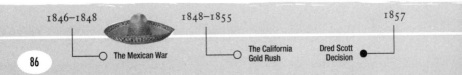

1846–1848   1848–1855   1857

The Mexican War   The California Gold Rush   Dred Scott Decision

no-brainer for white families that wanted to live a little bit of the good life. With the failure of the North to recognize the wisdom of slavery, a constant battle between the Northerners and the "black labor is good but black slavery is better" Southerners played out daily around the country.

I'm in No Rush to Get Back to Work

Citing the death of his master, army surgeon John Emerson, slave-turned-freedom-seeker Dred Scott decided to plead his case for liberty in front of the Missouri courts. Scott argued that he was actually a free citizen due to his fortuitous stays in Illinois and Wisconsin Territory, where slavery was barred under the Northwest Ordinance and the Missouri Compromise. Initially, his position was accepted by a lower St. Louis county court; however, on appeal, the Missouri State Supreme Court disagreed. The court ordered Scott, his wife, their kids, and the family dog, Liberty, back into the life of slavery. With the fight for freedom still raging and in no hurry to work in the fields for someone else's benefit, perpetual slacker Scott appealed the decision to the United States Supreme Court.

The Fix Was In

At the time, the Supreme Court was not a respected judicial institution that citizens, slaves, and Indians could look to for unbiased decisions rooted in legal fact. It was much like it is today, a mechanism for legislating from the bench, where justices' decisions are based on the political wishes of the party that put them into their cozy lifetime appointment. Much like the modern-day Supreme Court's ruling in favor of recovering alcoholic and great executioner George W. Bush in the 2000 presidential election, Scott's decision broke down along party lines. On March 6, 1857, the U.S. Supreme Court ruled against

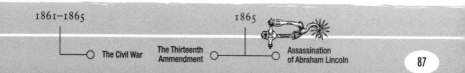

1861–1865   1865

Dred Scott and his bid for freedom. ☞ *Unfortunately for Scott, this fight was fixed, and Don King wasn't even involved.* ✏

Dismissed with Extreme Prejudice

Writing for the majority, eighty-year-old former slave owner turned Chief Justice Roger Taney ruled that blacks were not citizens and therefore Scott and his kind had no rights to petition the court for anything from Pop Tarts to freedom. He concluded that blacks "are so inferior that they had no rights which a white man was bound to respect." Feeling his prejudicial juices flowing, Taney trumped the whole "blacks are not citizens" play with a "blacks are so not citizens they are actually property" play. This meant that the owning of blacks was protected by the Fifth Amendment, no matter what state you lived in, thereby putting Dred and his dog Liberty on equal footing.

The fallout of Taney's ruling was that all legislative compromises were now off the table. The Supreme Court had ruled that blacks were property, not citizens, and white people could own 'em, breed 'em, and beat 'em. The only way the Northern states could prove that with a little sunscreen white and black skins were created equal in the mind of their God, was to get that written into the Constitution. Unfortunately, the South didn't just disagree, they strongly disagreed, and it ultimately required the death of 600,000 Americans to twist their arms to begrudgingly see the light. Following the North's Civil War victory, this change was put into the Constitution, and Liberty was demoted on the family totem pole.

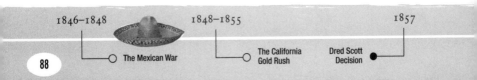

1846–1848   1848–1855   1857

The Mexican War   The California Gold Rush   Dred Scott Decision

THE CIVIL WAR

Different from "marital compromise," this one didn't involve going without sex for long periods of time

The War That Pitted Brother vs. Brother—about the Bruthas

Eighty-five years after the Founding Fathers signed the Declaration of Independence, all hell broke loose. The Union consisted of thirty-four states that were deeply divided. The central issue that threw the country into civil war was whether oral activities met the definition of sex in the new Union, and to a lesser degree, the issue of slavery.

The Southern states argued that slavery was a necessary ingredient to sustain the profitability of their many farming communities. Really, how can anyone expect you to pay a fair wage and still give your white wife and kids the lifestyle they deserve? No need getting your hands dirty working in the fields when God made you white. He had options when you were born and obviously felt you were qualified to manage a staff of black slaves.

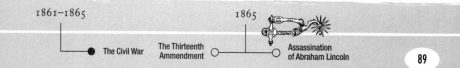

1861–1865

1865

The Civil War

The Thirteenth Ammendment

Assassination of Abraham Lincoln

On the other hand, the more economically advanced economy of the North wanted no part of slavery. Northerners had adopted the philosophy of all men being created equal. Yes men; women were way behind the equality curve at this time. ☞ *The exceptions were men from New York and Boston, where even today they continue to argue their superiority.* ☜

Unfortunately for the South, the sixteenth president of the United States was Abraham Lincoln, from Illinois. Lincoln, whose mug shot you can now find on the penny, was philosophically against the concept of slavery for the United States and had designs to emancipate his brothers from another mother. These divisions in philosophy, economic policy, and definitions of sex laid the groundwork for the deadliest battle in American history.

The Civil War Begins

Prior to bullets flying in 1861, the government attempted to defuse the conflict over slavery throughout the Union by allowing each incoming state to vote on whether to operate as a slave state, a free state, or as a Michael Jackson-influenced State of Shock. This half-assed attempt to encourage peace was known as the Compromise of 1850. Different from "marital compromise," this one didn't involve going without sex for long periods of time or scheduling erections for Tuesdays and Saturdays only. By not mandating a federal position on slavery and allowing each state to vote individually on whether it would act as a slave state or a free state, it was reasoned that each state would be content, and future issues would be eased. The reality was that Lincoln was buying time, waiting for his new recruits to graduate from his "Free the Black Man" military camps.

With tensions boiling, South Carolina reacted to Lincoln's objections to slavery by announcing its intent to secede from the Union. Quickly Mississippi, Florida, Georgia, Louisiana, and Texas followed suit. The "New South"

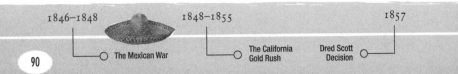

1846–1848   1848–1855   1857

The Mexican War   The California Gold Rush   Dred Scott Decision

was named the Confederacy. Jefferson Davis was named the president of the Confederacy and thereby automatically elevated to sacred status for generations of Southern kids who like to play with bed sheets, crosses, and fire.

On April 12, 1861, Davis's troops fired the first shots in Fort Sumter, South Carolina. Immediately, Arkansas, North Carolina, Virginia, and Tennessee joined the Confederacy, and the war was on! With an immense amount of passion for Jack Daniels, NASCAR, and chewing tobacco, the Confederacy took a significant advantage at the start of the war. The South used its veteran leadership to score victories at the Battle of Bull Run, the Second Battle of Bull Run, Fredericksburg, and Chancellorsville, but ☞ *like an eighty-year-old in the sack, the South just couldn't quite finish off what they had started.* ✑

Gettysburg, Where's That?

On July 1, 1863, Lee invaded Pennsylvania. Before coming into contact with Northern soldiers, Lee let his men overrun some Amish settlements as a confidence-builder. With the Amish vanquished, the Southern troops marched on. Northern forces met General Lee and his men for a battle at the now-famous Pennsylvania town of Gettysburg. Gettysburg was pivotal to the outcome of the war, as it was speculated that if the North had lost at Gettysburg, it would have negotiated a compromise allowing the Southern states to form their own separate country.

At the time, the British were making plans to jump into the war and assist the South, but being the frontrunners they are, they canceled those plans after the South's defeat at Gettysburg. The French also considered a similar strategy, but ran scared after reports of the beating the South endured at Gettysburg. Instead the French sent Le Coq Sportif gear and replica Eiffel towers

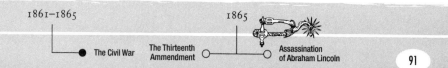

1861–1865   1865

The Civil War The Thirteenth Ammendment Assassination of Abraham Lincoln to inspire the Southern boys. Is it any wonder why so many people hate the French?

The South Surrenders, Reconstruction Begins

On April 2, 1865, the Southern capital of Richmond fell to General Grant. One week later, with a new fondness and appreciation for the black man, General Lee surrendered to General Grant at the Appomattox Court House. This action effectively ended the Civil War. All told, more than 600,000 Americans died during the War Between the States, by far the deadliest war in American history. Following the end of the war there was only one thing to do: rebuild.

In President Lincoln's Second Inaugural Address, he promised to "bind the nation's wounds." His philosophy was to restore the Union fully, and bear no grudge toward the Southern states. However, Lincoln never got a chance to heal the wounds of the young nation. Former Confederate and "oral is sex" supporter John Wilkes Booth assassinated him on April 14, 1865.

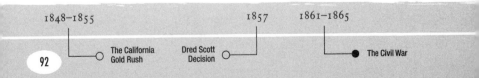

1848–1855   1857   1861–1865

The California Gold Rush   Dred Scott Decision   The Civil War

If you are unsure of which side you would have joined had you been alive during the Civil War, or if you are from one of those pesky border states, we have compiled a self-scoring exam to help you determine if you belong on the side of the North or the South. If you correctly score yourself on this page, you are ready to go ahead and attempt to score with others.

TRUE OR FALSE:

1. I truly believe the South won the Civil War, and will rise again.

2. I think prisons are built as affordable housing for black men.

3. I'm friends with a black guy who makes more money than I do and I'm okay with it.

4. Men only: I often wear overalls without a shirt underneath.

5. I know where to buy fitted white bed sheets with holes in them for my arms.

6. My ancestors and I consider other human beings who differed from us in any way to be property.

7. I think Rodney King got what he deserved.

8. I think Ron Goldman's wounds were self-inflicted.

9. The black women I would consider having a relationship with extends beyond Halle Berry.

10. Anytime I donate to the World Wildlife Fund I ask that my donation be returned if any of it gets earmarked to save the Black Panther.

11. I truly enjoy watching cars make left turns. I also consider these turn-lefters "athletes."

12. I drink whiskey named "Rebel Yell."

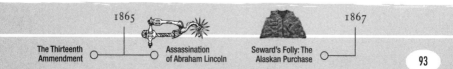

1865

The Thirteenth
Ammendment

Assassination
of Abraham Lincoln

Seward's Folly: The
Alaskan Purchase

1867

13. I fit into the stereotypes for both the common redneck, and his lesser known cousin, the Florida redneck.

14. I had no problem with Mr. Drummond's decision to take in Arnold and Willis in spite of the fact they were two black kids and he was a single white father living in Manhattan.

15. I tell the neighborhood kids that thunder occurs when God tells black people to move their furniture to their own side of heaven.

If you answered "true" to 1, 2, 4, 5, 6, 10, 11, 12, 13, or 15, you would call the South home-sweet-home.

If you answered "true" to 3, 9, or 14, you are a Northerner.

If you answered "true" to 7 or 8, you're likely unable to perform day-to-day activities on your own, including feeding and clothing yourself, and are a drain on the system.

If you are answered "true" to both Northern and Southern traits, immediately move yourself to purgatory-on-Earth, otherwise known as Eastern Kentucky.

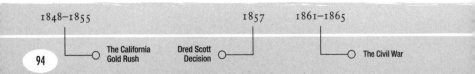

1848–1855   1857   1861–1865

The California Gold Rush   Dred Scott Decision   The Civil War

1865

THE THIRTEENTH AMENDMENT

Allows fraternity-like hazing techniques that include the naked human pyramid

Viewing Slavery Through Green-Tinted Glasses

Much to the dismay of Southern economists, Abraham Lincoln saw his dream of former slaves running free in the streets across America come true with the passage of the Thirteenth Amendment. Proponents of abolishing slavery focused solely on the humanitarian side of slavery. They argued that slavery was archaic and abusive and served no purpose in the land of opportunity. On the other hand, those who lived in the South and were white realized that slavery was a luxury that most of them didn't want to live without. Slaves were like eager chore-completing children, only older and more productive. One black man could do the work of twelve children at a fraction of the cost.

1865
The Thirteenth
Ammendment

Assassination
of Abraham Lincoln

Seward's Folly: The
Alaskan Purchase

1867

Free at Last, Free at Last

Issued at the ass end of the Civil War, Lincoln's Emancipation Proclamation had set most work-for-free blacks out on their own, unprepared to pursue a life of liberty. Slavery however, remained legal in the five states of New Jersey, Maryland, Missouri, Kentucky, and Delaware. The governor of Kentucky had refused to set the slaves of his state free in an effort to protect them from black-on-black crime. He believed he was doing blacks a favor by keeping them employed by their white owners and protecting them from each other.

Despite the Kentucky governor's best effort, the amendment to abolish slavery was ratified on December 6, 1865, leaving state legislators scrambling to build larger prisons. A poorly timed hunting expedition to Africa by the local KKK Chapter allowed Georgia to be the twenty-seventh state to pass the proposed amendment, giving Lincoln the required number of states he needed to set all black people free. The Cliff Notes to the Thirteenth Amendment reads:

> *Neither slavery nor involuntary servitude, except as a punishment for crime whereof the party shall have been duly convicted, shall exist within the United States, or any place subject to their jurisdiction*

Loose Interpretation

During the second term of George W. Bush's presidency, former attorney general and torture supporter Alberto Gonzales authored another one of his not-for-your-eyes memos informing the office of the president it was authorized to interpret the portion of the Thirteenth Amendment that states "any place

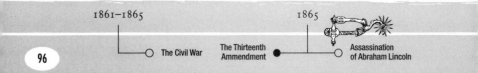

1861–1865   1865

The Civil War   The Thirteenth Ammendment   Assassination of Abraham Lincoln subject to their jurisdiction" to apply to all fifty states, the District of Columbia, Puerto Rico, as well as Afghanistan and Iraq.

☞ *With a lack of slavery found in Afghanistan and Iraq, Vice President/President Cheney asked Gonzales if the Thirteenth Amendment could also be interpreted to include the right to use coercive interrogation techniques.* ☜ Upon review, the White House's legal yes man Gonzales told Cheney that his interpretation of the Thirteenth Amendment allows fraternity-like hazing techniques that include sleep deprivation, loud noises, and naked human pyramids.

Racism Is Like Losing Weight

The passing of the Thirteenth Amendment in 1865 may have abolished slavery, but it didn't cure the racial problems in America. The open-minded free thinkers in the Mississippi legislature did not ratify the amendment until 1995, 130 years after it was initially passed. Those crazy white Baptists even repealed Prohibition in 1965, thirty years after the rest of the country. ☞ *Needless to say, racial hatred is like the last few pounds you put on during college: the hardest to get rid of.* ☜

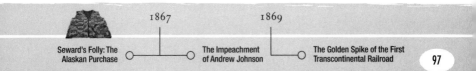

1867

Seward's Folly: The
Alaskan Purchase

1869

The Impeachment
of Andrew Johnson

The Golden Spike of the First
Transcontinental Railroad

97

1865

ASSASSINATION OF ABRAHAM LINCOLN

All pimped out in a Christian Dior white dress shirt, tuxedo jacket, and black top hat in preparation for the theatre

Friday Night and the Feeling's Right

Friday night is traditionally date night at the White House, and April 14, 1865, was no different. President Honest Abe Lincoln got all pimped out in a Christian Dior white dress shirt, tuxedo jacket, and black top hat in preparation for taking his wife, Mary Todd, out to see the hit comedy *Our America* playing at the downtown Ford's Theatre in Washington, D.C. Ever since Lincoln was sworn in as president, he had used these types of opportunities to win favor with his wife in the hopes of getting some late-night action without having to pull out the "I'm the commander and chief and I order you to remove your clothes and let me have colonial missionary-style sex with you" card.

☞ *With sex with his nimble Mary on the line and the long and deadly Civil War at its end, Lincoln was saying all the right things that Friday afternoon.* ☜ He was preaching for loving, one-on-one hus-

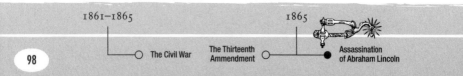

1861–1865

1865

The Civil War

The Thirteenth Ammendment

Assassination of Abraham Lincoln

band-and-wife relationships filled with foreplay-rich sex, along with reconciliation with the defeated slave-owning states of the South.

The Play was Murdered by the Critics

Later that evening, Abe and Mary Todd arrived at the theatre with their invited guests, Major Henry Rathbone and his young and sexy bride-to-be, Clara Harris. Abe had decided earlier in the week that if Mary Todd refuted his advancements he would pull the "I'm the commander and chief and I order you to remove your clothes and let me have dirty extramarital colonial missionary-style sex with you" card on the young and attractive Harris.

The president, his not always accommodating wife, the major, and his fiancée were sitting in a private box above the theatre stage that night. Just as one of the actors on stage was delivering the hi-fucking-larious line of "Wal, I guess I know enough to turn you inside out, you sockdologizing old mantrap," John Wilkes Booth shot President Abraham Lincoln. With all the hysterical laughter going on throughout the theatre, Lincoln's posse did not realize that the man who was about to give black America their freedom was bleeding to death.

Once the laughter subsided, the major looked over at Lincoln and realized he was suffering from what appeared to be a non-self-inflicted gunshot wound. This assessment was further solidified when he noticed the menacing JWB standing in the private box. ☞ *After proper introductions and an exchange of e-mail addresses, JWB jumped out of the box, catching the right spur of his boot on a flag.* ☜ As gravity took over, he dropped to the stage floor, breaking his left leg and shattering his New Year's resolution to exercise more.

Before limping off the stage, JWB flashed his weapon of choice and hollered out the state of Virginia's motto "Sic semper tyrannis!" meaning "thus

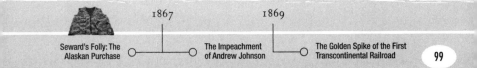

ever unto tyrants." Booth did not stick around to see if his words were favorably received or not. Instead, he quietly slipped out the back door and mounted his getaway horse.

Sic Semper to Self-Important Actors, Asshole

With the president in bad shape, he was quickly removed from the theatre and taken to a boarding house across the street. The next morning, the gunshot wound proved to be fatal, and the sixteenth president of the United States was pronounced dead. With Lincoln dead and the assassin on the loose, John Walsh of *America's Most Wanted* announced a $50,000 bounty on the head of JWB. In addition to the manhunt, friends, relatives, acquaintances, and struggling actors who might have known JWB were all arrested and thrown into Abu Ghraib where they were forced to don dog leashes for the entertainment of the guards.

Twelve days later, on his twenty-seventh birthday, JWB was sold out by a snitch within the Union Army. After expressing his lack of interest in surrendering, JWB was shot dead by an army soldier.

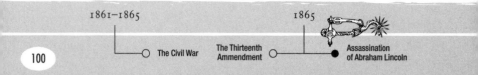

1861–1865

1865

The Civil War

The Thirteenth
Ammendment

Assassination
of Abraham Lincoln

SEWARD'S FOLLY: THE ALASKAN PURCHASE

Purchased for $7.2 million, two pairs of jeans, and a signed Marilyn Monroe poster

Alaska: The Polar Bear Garden

Originally, the United States thought they had won the frozen, snow-covered land that topographers now refer to as Alaska in a late-night poker game. Secretary of State William Seward had bet all of the land the Native Americans had left on a second pair with top kicker. Screw it—it wasn't his land. He reasoned if he lost, he could trade for it from the Indians for a few feather necklaces and some fancy beads.

Surprisingly, the Russian Foreign Minister to the United States, Louis Baydalal, welshed on the bet and instead offered Seward one mail-order bride. Shortly after Natasha was delivered, Baydalal came clean with Seward, telling him in 1867 that Russia was low on rubles and they needed to sell the 586,412 square miles of ice. Fortunately for the desperate Russians, Seward was an excitable expansionist and blood rushed to his groin at the thought of

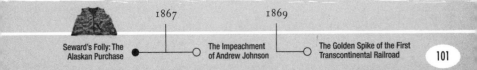

1867   1869

Seward's Folly: The Alaskan Purchase   The Impeachment of Andrew Johnson   The Golden Spike of the First Transcontinental Railroad   101

the United States acquiring more territory, regardless of its harsh climate and distance from the contiguous states.

Focused on ensuring that the British did not acquire the land, the Russians were prepared to accept nearly any deal the United States offered. Capitalizing on Seward's shrewd negotiating skills, the United States purchased the land for $7.2 million, two pairs of jeans, and a signed Marilyn Monroe poster for the Russian Emperor Alexander II. All in all, the nearly 600,000-square-mile polar bear playground was acquired for approximately 1.9 cents an acre.

At first, the general public gave Seward props for the purchase. War-weary Americans were supportive anytime they could acquire more land without the hassle of burying the dead from another armed conflict. This sentiment, however, was not shared with everyone in the media. Some newspaper editors criticized the purchase as being a huge mistake, believing that the land was not worth taking, even if the Russians were giving it away. Several newspapers led with satirical headlines like "Seward's Folly" and "Seward's Icebox."

Alaska's Bosom Is Stacked with Natural Resources

Seward's critics were short lived, as a little more than three decades later, large quantities of gold were found in Alaska. This discovery made the purchase price easier to swallow, and not spit as Seward was praised for his foresight. To the disappointment of our Arab oil brokers, today Alaska produces about 20 percent of the nation's oil, with vast untapped oil reserves remaining off limits within a wildlife refuge.

Most importantly, Alaska gave 2008 Republican vice presidential nominee Sarah Palin the foreign policy experience necessary to be president. As Palin pointed out, she governed a state that is only a short distance from Russia.

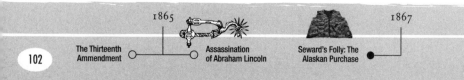

1865

1867

The Thirteenth
Ammendment

Assassination
of Abraham Lincoln

Seward's Folly: The
Alaskan Purchase

☞ *With only sixteen miles separating the two countries' nearest points, when Putin visits the area and the sun shines just right, she can see the whites of President Dmitry Medvedev's puppet masters eyes.* ☜ "Tell me if Senator Joe Biden can do that from his perch in Delaware," she often boastfully asked during campaign stops.

Luckily for Putin, Palin and the Republicans lost the 2008 election, ensuring that when he and his comrades visit the popular sixteen miles of separation, they can continue to take bets on whether Palin has Cs or Ds hidden under her hunting vest.

The Impeachment of Andrew Johnson

His inability to work well with others in the congressional sandbox directly led to his impeachment trial

Lucky Number 17

Around the White House, President Abraham Lincoln could often be heard mumbling, "guns don't kill people, people kill people." And on April 14, 1865, it wasn't the bullet that left Lincoln dead, it was the triggerman John Wilkes Booth that ended the life of the sitting president, effectively handing the job of commander in chief to the even less attractive, less qualified, and less popular vice president, Mr. Andrew Johnson from the volunteer state of Tennessee.

☞ *Following Lincoln's death, Johnson was quickly installed as the seventeenth and least sexy president of the land of the free and home of the brave.* ✑ His loud and obnoxious nature made him widely unpopular in all political circles, including the ones within his own home. Using his inability to win friends and influence people against himself, Johnson found his ability to govern effectively to be satisfyingly difficult.

1865

Assassination of Abraham Lincoln

Seward's Folly: The Alaskan Purchase

1867

The Impeachment of Andrew Johnson

As America's deadliest war came to an end and reconstruction began, those who favored inept leadership were ecstatic with Johnson's efforts. Unlike Lincoln, who spoke openly about not punishing the Confederate South, Johnson preferred a more tempered approach to forgiveness. Johnson's strategy of forgiveness with conditions was wildly unpopular on both sides of the issue. He walked around the oval office with a hard on every time he stirred the pot with a civil rights veto. It was Johnson's continued inability to work well with others in the congressional sandbox that directly led to his history-making impeachment trial.

Maybe the Third Time Is the Charm

In November of 1867, C-SPAN began beaming their gavel-to-gavel coverage of Johnson's impeachment trial into the homes of dozens. After several days of uneventful and unsatisfying sloppy oral debate, a vote on Johnson's removal was held on December 5, 1867, in the House of Representatives. Once it was clear that even a hanging chad controversy could not overturn the failed impeachment hearing, Johnson went back to the White House to celebrate his continued authority over the United States.

A second attempt to remove President Johnson from office took place in 1868 when he was charged with violating the Tenure of Office Act. This poorly understood act nearly allowed congressional hatred to succeed in removing the president from the comfortable surroundings of the oval office. ☞ *This time, after all the votes were counted, host of C-SPAN idol Ryan Seacrest announced before a live television audience, "Congress has voted and by a margin of one vote, Andrew, you are safe."* ☜ This single vote kept President Johnson in the oval office, only further fueling the resentment and hatred of both sides.

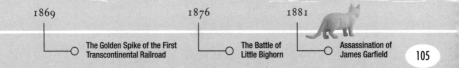

1869
1876
1881

The Golden Spike of the First
Transcontinental Railroad

The Battle of
Little Bighorn

Assassination of
James Garfield

105

Blind Pig Finds an Ear of Corn

When his time as president came to a close, Johnson scored historically low both in approval ratings and on the "Is he hot or not?" board in the town square. A complete failure in terms of his presidency, Johnson's most important and perhaps only success was his purchase of Alaska from the soon-to-be free-will-restricted Communist nation of the Russia. Without this international land transfer deal, American oil reserves would be embarrassingly low, and the pool of female vice president candidates would be less physically attractive.

1865   Assassination of Abraham Lincoln   Seward's Folly: The Alaskan Purchase   1867   The Impeachment of Andrew Johnson

THE GOLDEN SPIKE OF THE FIRST TRANSCONTINENTAL RAILROAD

How to get rich quick using no-bid government contracts

Nonlubricated Penetration

The wildly successful Trail of Tears served as the backdrop for spearheading an effort to link the eastern United States with the more laid-back western states as suddenly compassionate legislators everywhere demanded that the country be linked by rails. It was argued that the effort to move the Indians out west by foot decades earlier proved to be too time consuming, and although they were indifferent about the many deaths, they rationalized that if they ever needed to relocate another ethnic group in the future, they needed to prepare for it well in advance. In looking at the wave of unruly immigrants moving into the country, it became apparent the railroad system would serve a much greater purpose than simply moving important business commodities—it would act as an on-call ethnic people shuffler.

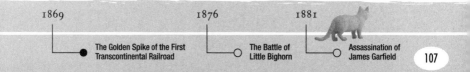

The East-West Gravy Train

Of course, when legislators get sudden compassion for a cause, it can only mean one thing: there is money to be made. After receiving former Vice President Dick Cheney's Halliburton-sponsored audiotapes on how to get rich quick using no-bid government contracts, Oakes Ames, a prominent and successful shovel manufacturer and congressman, gathered up a handful of the most financially privileged Americans and British to begin a private effort to build the iron minority mover. Ames took the Halliburton system to new heights as he influenced the United States government to not only give them the land to build the railroad, but also give them huge amounts of additional land to sell on their own, ensuring their profitability.

In Halliburton-like fashion, several individuals made fortunes, while the rest of the country had the pleasure of paying nearly twice as much as expected for the completed railway. For many, this seemed impossible, as the east-to-west portion of the track was mostly laid by hungover Irish immigrants and the west-to-east track was laid mostly by Chinese immigrants who were still weak from their journey, all of whom earned slave-like wages at best.

Aiding the investors' efforts to realize huge profits were towns all across the country that paid huge bribes to the railroad companies to convince them of the merits of running the railroad through their town. These eagerly accepted bribes resulted in many twists and turns, inconveniently changing the path of the transcontinental rails.

Don't Sign a Gym Membership

On May 10, 1869, the ethnic people shuffler was completed when railroad profiteer Leland Stanford drove in a ceremonial golden spike that effectively connected the eastern portion of the United States to the western portion of

1867

1869

Seward's Folly: The
Alaskan Purchase

The Impeachment
of Andrew Johnson

The Golden Spike of the First
Transcontinental Railroad

the United States. This was a relief to compassionate legislators, as they now had a more humane way of taking conveniently located, fertile land from ethnic landowners and exchanging it for less fertile, more inconveniently located land elsewhere in the country. It also ensured that if some great resource was discovered in the Indians' new home, we could move them again. But this time if we needed the exchanged land that was given to Native Americans with the Indian Removal Act back again, we would not force them to walk hundreds of miles to their new government-approved location, providing they could afford the train ticket.

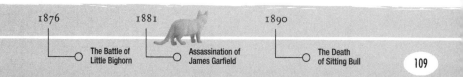

1876

1881

1890

The Battle of
Little Bighorn

Assassination of
James Garfield

The Death
of Sitting Bull

THE BATTLE OF LITTLE BIGHORN

The largest fiasco in American military history

Put a Dollar in the Loincloth

Americans have always taken great pride in their ability to run profitable strip clubs in a country founded on Judeo-Christian principles along with their ability to succeed militarily on the battlefield. The Little Bighorn River, located in Montana, may have been without a gentlemen's club in 1876, however, it did prove to be an appropriate venue for George Custer's last stand. Over the years, Custer's last stand has fondly become known as perhaps the largest fiasco in American military history.

Custer-Filled Rumley

He was born George "I'll go down in history" Custer in New Rumley, Ohio, famous for, well, Custer being born there. Custer was an embarrassment to

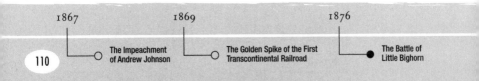

1867 — The Impeachment of Andrew Johnson

1869 — The Golden Spike of the First Transcontinental Railroad

1876 — The Battle of Little Bighorn

New Rumley, as he graduated from West Point academy dead last in his class. His ineptness extending beyond the classroom, Custer performed miserably once on duty. He was court-martialed, only to be saved from punishment by the timely outbreak of the Civil War and the shortage of trained soldiers. After being court-martialed a second time, Custer was assigned to be part of the 1876 mission to take down the Lakota tribe along with the more competent Generals Gibbon and Crook.

A Horse, a Bull, and a Crook Go into a Bar . . .

In 1876, the U.S. government ordered the Lakota chiefs to report to their designated land by the end of January. ☞ *Ignoring Native Americans' claim that they were there first, the federal government was kind enough to make additional room for white people by ordering the Indians to take up residency in a little space out west that the whites didn't want yet.* ☜

Sitting Bull and Crazy Horse, among others, decided not to comply. Generals Gibbon and Crook were sent with Custer to drive Sitting Bull and the other chiefs onto the reservation for a lifetime of gambling and alcohol. As the fight began, Crazy Horse and his warriors got the upper hand, forcing General Crook to retreat. Later in June, Custer found Sitting Bull's encampment near the Little Bighorn River. Sensing an historic opportunity, Custer disregarded the original plan and instead charged ahead only to find out that he and his men were outnumbered four-to-one. Needless to say, Custer's premonition about history was correct. The Lakota warriors killed Custer and all of his troops, offering no surrender. It was one of the worst defeats in U.S. military history. Despite more troops coming later for Sitting Bull, he and his men escaped to Canada where their native style of dress and incomprehensible speech made them nearly invisible.

1881 — Assassination of James Garfield

1890 — The Death of Sitting Bull

1901 — Assassination of William McKinley

On Common Ground

For his efforts, history has not forgotten the foolish way in which General George Custer died, and fittingly, numerous cemeteries have been named after him. ☞ *As for Crazy Horse, history remembers him too, with numerous strip clubs around the country carrying his name.* ◁ It is nice to see that after all of the blood, death, and tears there is still an environment that both Judeo-Christian white men and descendents of fierce Indian warriors can enjoy together.

1867 — The Impeachment of Andrew Johnson

1869 — The Golden Spike of the First Transcontinental Railroad

1876 — The Battle of Little Bighorn

ASSASSINATION OF JAMES GARFIELD

Having never before been assassinated, the new experience intrigued Garfield

Decidedly Undecided

James Garfield was indifferent about the distinction of being the twentieth president of the United States. Those who knew him best and those who never knew him at all have debated whether he was afflicted with a bad case of Attention Deficit Disorder or if he simply had issues making up his mind. His inability to focus on any one given task was legendary. Garfield was born on November 19, 1831, in Orange, Ohio, after considering exiting the womb in several different cities.

Garfield's inability to make decisions developed when he was a young child; however, it wasn't until he entered college that it really started to show. He accepted admission into Western Reserve Eclectic Institute, seemingly the perfect place for the inattentive Garfield, considering their unique mix of

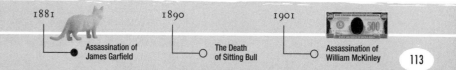

1881
Assassination of
James Garfield

1890
The Death
of Sitting Bull

1901
Assassination of
William McKinley

113

studies. As expected, Garfield got bored and he transferred to Williams College in Massachusetts, where, predictably, he changed majors constantly.

Upon graduation, Garfield couldn't muster up a decision on an occupation, so he defaulted with God and became a minister at the Franklin Circle Christian Church. Quickly deciding he wasn't as religious as he first thought, he quit on God in an unsuccessful attempt to become a high school principal in Poestenkill, New York. Unsatisfied and lost, he bailed on the principal experiment to become a teacher at the aptly named Eclectic Institute for the 1856–1857 academic year. Still feeling unfulfilled, he took over as the University's president from 1857 to 1860.

In 1858, he married Lucretia Rudolph, but unable to decide on one woman, he dallied with Lucia Calhoun, and then decided he was right the first time and went back to his wife. Next, Garfield decided that the academic life wasn't for him and became a lawyer, passing the Ohio bar in 1860. Waiting for his entrance into the bar, he became unsure if legal work was for him and became an Ohio State Senator from 1859 to 1861. Confused but determined, he tried stints as a major general in the U.S. Army, a member of the U.S. House of Representatives, and a member of the Electoral Commission in 1876. Still trying to find himself, he experimented with the job of the U.S. president in 1880.

Indecision Maker

During the election of 1880, things were hotly contested. Garfield ran as the Republican nominee, and Winfield Scott Hancock ran as the Democratic candidate. Following the vote, the wiser more important Electoral College decisively installed Garfield as the president of the United States by a margin of 214 votes to 155, despite the popular vote being only 10,000 votes apart. The victory made the successful and indecisive Garfield an acting congressman, senator elect, and president elect. Obviously, Garfield liked to keep his

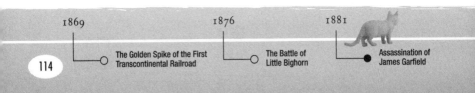

1869 — The Golden Spike of the First Transcontinental Railroad

1876 — The Battle of Little Bighorn

1881 — Assassination of James Garfield

career options open. But whether or not he would become bored with being the president, we would never find out.

Dead or Alive?

If presidents received an official letter grade, Bush Jr. would get an "F," Reagan a B+, Carter a "D," and Garfield an "I" as he was president for only four months before being killed. ☞ *ON July 2, 1881, lasagna hater and lawyer Charles Guiteau shot President Garfield at a train station.* ☜ Guiteau apparently thought he should be in line for employment in a cushy position as consul in Paris. Garfield naturally couldn't make up his mind on who should fill the position, and despite Guiteau's protests, Garfield moved on to not decide on other equally important issues. When his protestation fell on deaf ears, Guiteau made sure his last protest rang out in the form of a revolver shot. Having never before been assassinated, the new experience intrigued Garfield. He experienced both the wound and the fascination of it all for four weeks before deciding he had done it all and tried one last experience, being bored to death. Garfield died on September 19, 1881.

1890

1901

1913

The Death
of Sitting Bull

Assassination of
William McKinley

Income Tax
Enacted

1890

THE DEATH OF
SITTING BULL

Whites have long been considered the lowest on the getting-down totem pole

Dance by Numbers

With absolutely no shame, white America happily forces the Macarena, the electric slide, and the chicken dance on naive and impressionable dancing enthusiasts at weddings and professional sporting events. Children with white parents and white parents with white parents have turned their backs on common decency and actively participated in these childishly scripted dances on the pretense that it strengthens the fabric of America. ☞ *DANCES LIKE THESE ARE HEAVILY PROMOTED BY WHITE AMERICA, AS THEY GIVE MANY OF THE RHYTHMICALLY CHALLENGED THE OPPORTUNITY TO FEEL SAFE AND SECURE ON THE DANCE FLOOR.* ◤ Now if they could only produce a step-by-step method to solve many a white man's problem with lack of endowment.

Capitalizing on the theory of strength in numbers, those dancers with a fair complexion now make their darker, more rhythmically inclined dancing

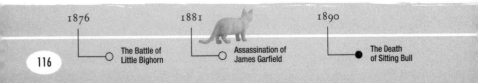

1876

The Battle of
Little Bighorn

1881

Assassination of
James Garfield

1890

The Death
of Sitting Bull

counterparts nervous. Whites have long been considered the lowest on the getting-down totem pole, and for scores of white Americans to confidently dance in public, it is clear that non-whites must lose their monopoly on the business of cuttin' the rug.

A Hot New Dance

The precedent for using dancing as a tool to create fear in those of a different complexion was laid out in the 1880s when Native Americans singing "this land is our land" offered up the Ghost Dance to their dance-hungry brothers and sisters. Similar to popular white dances, it was believed by those who believed that the dance had the support of God. In fact, it was believed, that if you believed, and God believed that you believed, then he would protect the believer from the bullets of the white man's gun. After years of constant battle with the White-non-Hispanic U.S. military the enthusiasm for being shot was at an all-time low in the Native American community.

Choreographers of the Ghost Dance used this lack of desire to be inflicted with gunshot wounds to raise the popularity of their hot new dance. The Ghost Dance received heavy rotation in the club scene between the regular rotation of 50 Cent and T-Pain tracks.

Death by Macarena

To give credibility to their dance, the choreographers signed a promotional deal with one of the most respected Native American military leaders, Sitting Bull. Sitting Bull was required to promote the Ghost Dance within his community and to lend his image for print and television advertisements. The well-liked Sitting Bull proved to be the right front man, as the popularity of the Ghost Dance spread like herpes at a condom-free swingers party.

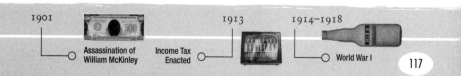

1901

Assassination of
William McKinley

1913

Income Tax
Enacted

1914–1918

World War I

By the end of 1890, the fear of the Ghost Dance within the white community reached historic proportions, reaching Number 2 on Whitey's Fear Chart, just behind being left alone in an alley with a large number of muscular men of African descent who had been abused by their slave owner. The fear resulted in the government agent responsible for keeping an eye on the wildly popular Sitting Bull to order his arrest.

On December 15, 1890, special agent James McLaughlin, fearful that there might be something to this "I believe and God believes I believe" rhetoric, cowardly ordered the Native American reservation police to arrest Sitting Bull. During the arrest, a Rodney King–like riot broke out, resulting in Sitting Bull being shot dead. With Sitting Bull dead from a gunshot wound, the Ghost Dance proved to not live up to all its hype. Native Americans everywhere were disappointed at this and began to turn their attention to a new dance craze, called "retreat to the reservation." ☞ *This tragedy aside, we can only be thankful there are not more casualties when large groups of white people take to the dance floor.* ☜

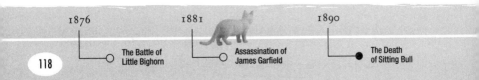

1876 — The Battle of Little Bighorn

1881 — Assassination of James Garfield

1890 — The Death of Sitting Bull

1901

Assassination of William McKinley

The president that nobody remembers

Horton Hears a "Who?"

William McKinley is the president that nobody remembers, family and friends included. Born in Ohio in 1843, this white shadow's hometown of Canton, Ohio, is far more famous for being the home of Pro Football's Hall of Fame than it is for being the birthplace of our twenty-fifth and most forgettable president. A Civil War veteran, McKinley steadily rose in rank, although nobody remembers why. As president, he may have been a proponent of the gold standard and possibly in favor of keeping tariffs high on imports, although he could have been for low tariffs and "Made in China" stickers on every toy—historians aren't sure.

☞ *McKinley had a "been there, done that, got the T-shirt" attitude toward being governor of Ohio in 1896.* ☜ Following his forgettable stint as governor, McKinley kept his low profile by winning the Republican

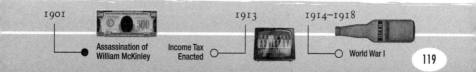

1901

Assassination of William McKinley

Income Tax Enacted

1913

1914–1918

World War I

119

nomination for president. His opponent, William Jennings Bryan, ran on one issue and one issue only: the issue of disqualifying the Hollywood foreign press from voting for the Oscars, condoms in the classroom, the fair tax, greenhouse emission controls, military reform, and same-sex unions. Despite Bryan's one-issue platform, he found it impossible to compete with McKinley's anonymity, as he followed the time-tested formula of military man + state governor = next president of the United States.

Who Killed the President?

McKinley's assassin is as anonymous as the president he murdered. Alongside fellow presidential assassins with names like John Wilkes Booth and Lee Harvey Oswald, the name of Leon Frank Czolgosz just doesn't have any sizzle. Like all presidential assassins, Czolgosz was an anarchist and a loner. Not using his nonrhythmic name as a crutch, Leon aborted his original plan of killing the president with a candlestick in the library in favor of the more traditional gun in front of scores of witnesses.

Czolgosz shot McKinley at the Pan Am Exposition being held in Buffalo, New York. Leon simply walked up to the president and calmly pulled out his pistol, shooting the president twice. After the shooting, the crowd beat Czolgosz, nearly killing him. Despite the crowd's lack of follow through, the courts finished what they started, as Czolgosz was executed in the electric chair in October 1901.

Who Was That Man?

As for the legacy of the dead McKinley, it is the legacy of the forgotten president. He quietly and uneventfully passed away from the gunshot wounds eight days after the shooting. As a symbolic gesture of remembrance, the government

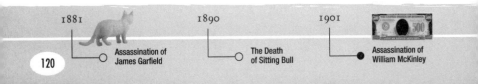

1881 — Assassination of James Garfield

1890 — The Death of Sitting Bull

1901 — Assassination of William McKinley

named a mountain after McKinley in the far off and nearly uninhabitable state of Alaska. In keeping with McKinley's forgettableness, many Alaskans simply refer to the mountain by its Native American name, Denali.

After his death, Americans felt they had awakened from a case of amnesia, as McKinley was succeeded by Theodore Roosevelt, a much more memorable president in Americans' minds. ☞ *But in honoring McKinley by putting him on the $500 bill, we have assured that most Americans will never know the face of our twenty-fifth president William McKinley.* ✑

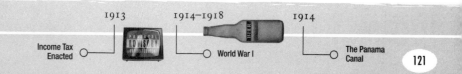

1913

INCOME TAX ENACTED

Through the magic of the IRS, American workers have the opportunity to help finance lavish White House dinners

Proud to Be an American

Over the years, Americans have been fortunate to have numerous opportunities to be proud of their country and its citizens, both natural and naturalized. Starting out with a handful of unwanted European castoffs that stormed the shores of the east coast of what is now the United States, they were able to convince tribe after tribe of Indians that they would enjoy the challenges of raising their families out west where the conditions for difficult farming were ideal. Through intimidation and near daily beatings, they were able to make use of unruly black labor to harvest cotton, tobacco, and sugarcane. ☞ *They were able to take a semiliterate actor named Sylvester Stallone, whose best dialogue consisted of grunting, and turn it into a six-film franchise.* ☜ And finally, through generations of careful designer

1890

1901

1913

The Death
of Sitting Bull

Assassination of
William McKinley

Income Tax
Enacted

breeding, America was able to give birth to an eager porn star named Houston, who excitedly set a modern day gangbang record in 1999 by having sex 620 times over the course of eight hours. America stood at attention and their pride swelled on that fateful day.

Even with all of these explosively satisfying moments, nothing makes hard-working Americans feel prouder than when they look at their pay stub every other week and see their automatic contribution to the Internal Revenue Service.

First Comes Love, Then Comes Marriage

Capitalizing on Americans' desire to fund government projects before funding their family bank accounts, the Sixteenth Amendment to the Constitution, ratified in 1913, provides the federal government the authority to levy taxes on personal income. This wildly popular amendment called for a progressive tax that allowed the highest earners the satisfaction of contributing an even greater proportion of their income to the beloved IRS. During the honeymoon stage, the income tax started at 1 percent of taxable income above $3,000 for individuals and 1 percent of taxable income above $4,000 for married couples, ensuring that a marriage penalty would always be part of the tax code and the honeymoon with the IRS would never end.

It is through the magic of the IRS that American workers have the opportunity to help finance freedom fighters in other countries, host lavish White House dinners for hated foreign dignitaries, and provide subsidies to insanely profitable oil companies to continue their willingness to sell us their products that we have come to love and cherish.

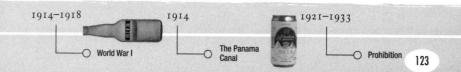

1914–1918   1914   1921–1933

World War I   The Panama Canal   Prohibition

Pay It Forward

Recognizing that wealthy people are very passionate about war and they are inherently philanthropic, the income tax levels were adjusted to call for top earners to contribute 77 percent of their income to the IRS during World War I and an orgasmically satisfying 91 percent during World War II. For many big-hearted rich Americans, the war ended too soon. With the scaled-back tax rates of peacetime that followed, many of the richest of the rich were left feeling a little charitable void in their life.

Fortunately for today's Americans, little has changed. The opportunity to participate financially in foreign conflicts is still mandatory. The rich are still given the opportunity to experience higher taxation rates. The marriage penalty is still in place and every once in a while we still get to pay for the food and entertainment of political leaders that hate us. ☞ *THE IRS: ScREWiNg you liKE A HoNEYmooN bRidE SiNcE 1913.* ☜

1890

The Death
of Sitting Bull

1901

Assassination of
William McKinley

Income Tax
Enacted

1913

WORLD WAR I

Both sides declined the invitation, choosing to have a meet and greet luncheon with Cameron Diaz instead

Shot Heard Round the World

Decades before the LA Bloods allegedly shot Notorious B.I.G. in retaliation for the murder of 2Pac, there was a slightly less memorable shot heard around the world when Archduke Francis Ferdinand was gunned down Compton-style by the Serbian Blood Gavrilo Princip while in Sarajevo in 1914.

Besides being the target of Blood-on-archduke violence, Ferdinand was the heir in waiting to the Austrian throne. ☞ *As Austrian royalty, the family of privilege enjoyed free lift tickets to the country's municipal ski resorts along with an assortment of "we've got your back" friendships from a handful of capitalism-crushing world leaders and their militaries.* ☜

With the orderly succession to the Austrian crown now out of succession and Princip's assassin behavior exposed, the Austrian military declared all out

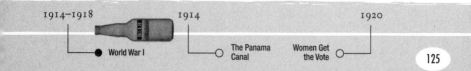

1914–1918

1914

1920

World War I

The Panama Canal

Women Get the Vote

Armageddon on Princip's home country of Serbia. Not without friends, the tiny nation of Serbia received military support from neighboring Russia. As Russian troops entered the fray, the first country to overreact to the ruble users' involvement and the archduke pushing daisies was the 1990 FIFA World Cup champion, Germany.

Enthusiastic to share the joys of war with other European countries, the Germans responded by checking off France, Serbia, and Russia on their Declaration of War paperwork. ☞ *As France became entangled in the web of war, the "soccer-is-football" nation of Great Britain eagerly declared war on Germany because of their friendship with France.* ☜

American Reaction

Coming off the heels of the American Revolutionary War of 1775–1783, the War of 1812, the Mexican War of 1846–1848, the American Civil War of 1861–1865, and the Spanish American War of 1898, the almost pacifist nation of the United States naturally played Swiss with the growing European conflict, openly expressing its neutrality. In an effort to mediate a quick resolution to the war, in August of 1914 the American government offered to send Judge Judy, and in case the Germans like African Americans more than women, Judge Mathis to Europe to negotiate a peace deal. Sensing the possibility of a near immediate victory, both sides declined the invitation, countering with their willingness to have a meet and greet luncheon with Cameron Diaz and Alyssa Milano instead.

Germany Tugs on Superman's Cape

As the diplomacy efforts of the United States failed to gain traction, the first significant battle got underway in September 1914. With a total disregard

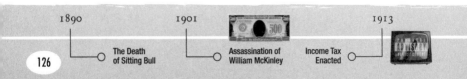

1890

1901

1913

126

The Death
of Sitting Bull

Assassination of
William McKinley

Income Tax
Enacted

for human life, the First Battle of the Marne became a huge killing field. Between the dead and injured, each side suffered over 500,000 casualties. ☞ *The French effort surprised Germany, as the "Drink Becks responsibly" Germans conceded the battle, leaving their late-at-night stroking fantasy of a quick and relatively resistant free takeover unfulfilled and unlikely.* ✍

Dissatisfied with their success on land, the German armed force began a water offensive despite the daunting naval superiority of the British. Rationalizing that the fun and games on water should not be restricted to military vessels alone, the Germans targeted Allied fare-paying passenger and commercial ships.

Testing America's desire to remain neutral was the U-boat assault and sinking of the British ocean liner *Lusitania* on May 7, 1915. Trapped in the death count were 128 American citizens. Reacting to the attack, President Woodrow Wilson commenced a letter-writing exchange campaign with the Germans, warning them against any form of continued aggression that included Americans. Hearing but not listening to the American rhetoric, the Germans sunk the U.S. commercial liner *Leelanaw* in the coastal region of Scotland on July 25, 1915. The American death toll took another hit when twenty-seven citizens of the stars and stripes met their untimely death at the hands of an Austrian submarine while aboard the Italian vessel *Ancona*. As the American death count continued to rise, the federal government began making plans to abandon their Swiss ambitions and enter the war.

America Enters Worldwide Orgy

Following the unprovoked sinking of five more seaworthy American vessels, Wilson went in front of Congress seeking a declaration of war on Germany. Realizing the profitable nature of war and how it could positively impact their

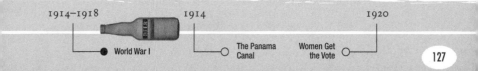

1914–1918   1914   1920

World War I   The Panama Canal   Women Get the Vote

districts, members of the house and senate voted overwhelmingly for participation in the Great War.

In an attempt to drum up the support of young American males, Congress passed the Selective Service Act on May 18, 1917, requiring all those fortunate enough to be between the ages of twenty-one and thirty to register for their right to be drafted and made into instant warriors. ☞ *Showing a great deal of enthusiasm for their chance to be selected to serve, 10 million men put pen to registration form, throwing their names into the I-can-dodge-bullets hat.* ☜ Unfortunately for many, only 2.8 million people enjoyed the thrill of being chosen from the long list of age-qualified candidates.

As the newly drafted American soldiers settled into the luxurious surroundings of war, the Russian military began pulling their troops out of the conflict, significantly reducing the number of available Allied combatants. With the Russians out and the battle-anxious Americans in, the tide of victory began to turn in favor of the Allied forces. In September 1918, nearly 900,000 mostly new-to-the-military Americans joined another 100,000 troops from the coalition of the winning in the Battle of the Argonne. Despite the heavy casualties suffered on the red, white, and blue side, the United States and their allies were victorious. Within weeks, the Germans waved a little white flag signing an armistice treaty to cease the killing at 11:00 A.M. on November 11, 1918.

With the conflict over and a blueprint for peace agreed to with the signing of the Treaty of Versailles on June 28, 1919, the announcements of the human cost associated with the reaction to the archduke's assassination were sobering. A combined total of over 13.5 million people died and over 21 million people were wounded. Most of the deceased had been leading regular civilian lives before Princip ended the life of the archduke. After everything was all over, people from around the world reflected on how things would have been different if the archduke had been without friends in June of 1914.

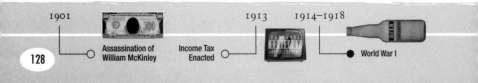

1901

Assassination of
William McKinley

Income Tax
Enacted

1913

1914–1918

World War I

THE PANAMA CANAL

A man-made waterway built by pastry chefs

Canal Knowledge

After the French predictably fumbled the ball, making a deadly mess out of their attempt to connect the Atlantic Ocean with the Pacific Ocean with a man-made waterway built by pastry chefs, the United States stepped in and picked up where the French failure left off.

Starting in 1880, France sent its most experienced éclair makers to Panama to begin construction of a forty-eight-mile-long birthing canal that would allow sea-weary sailors to avoid the trip around Cape Horn when attempting to ocean-hop from one to the other. For sailors who loved the scenery but not the sailing, a trip from New York to San Francisco was cut by 8,000 miles when using the Panama Canal.

1914 — The Panama Canal

1920 — Women Get the Vote

1921–1933 — Prohibition

Immunizations Anyone?

The idea for the canal dates as far back as the sixteenth century but it wasn't until the French showed their incompetence beginning in 1880 that anything really got started. Drawing on their egocentric yet underqualified and undermotivated workforce, the French government sent scores of soon-to-be quitters to the jungle and mountain ranges of Panama. With their spirits low and their ingenuity lower, the project quickly ran into many problems, not the least of which being the one-two-three punch of malaria, yellow fever, and a shortage of white wine. By 1889, the French had predictably given up.

America Takes Over

Ashamed of our French allies' results, President Theodore Roosevelt scolded the French prime minister for their continued tradition of running and hiding when things get tough and then bought the equipment they left behind in Panama for $40 million. John "Frank the Tank" Stevens was appointed chief engineer on the project. Stevens convinced Roosevelt that the canal needed to be a series of locks, which the French felt was an ugly and dirty solution, beneath their standards.

With a workable solution from an engineer perspective in place, the United States made a large investment to control the diseases that had devastated the French construction force. This effort resulted in the deaths of a much more manageable 5,600 workers. Once the disease issue was under control, work progressed much more swiftly. To the disappointment of the French, the canal was completed in 1914, a full two years ahead of schedule.

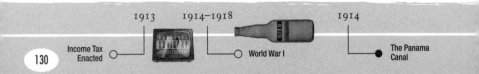

1913 — Income Tax Enacted

1914–1918 — World War I

1914 — The Panama Canal

With the Atlantic Ocean and Pacific Ocean now connected through a manmade canal that to this day stills gives Sheiks from Dubai a little wood for its engineering brilliance, trade around the world is easier than ever. The total American investment in the project was approximately $375 million. ☞ *At a campaign stop in Ohio during his re-election campaign, the fiscally responsible President George W. Bush was overheard saying, "For that price, they should have built two!"* ☜

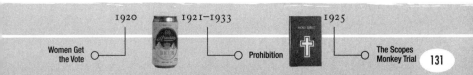

1920

WOMEN GET THE VOTE

Burning bras and hairy legs began to rise at an alarming rate

I Ain't Nobody

If a woman walked into a polling station on the second Tuesday in November of an election year in the early nineteenth century, she would be turned away. The mystic powers of the female may include a tendency to change their mind at a moments' notice and the ability to give birth, but it did not include participation in America's electoral process. The responsibility to ensure that only the most capable men were elected to shape government policy through democracy rested solely on the willing shoulders of American males.

Change of Position

Beginning in 1848, social reform hopefuls Elizabeth Cady Stanton and Lucretia Mott got out in front of women's quest for a devalued vote. It all

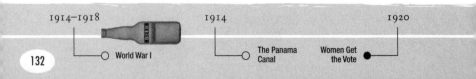

1914–1918   1914   1920

World War I   The Panama Canal   Women Get the Vote

started in 1840 when Mott and other women were denied being seated at the World Anti-Slavery Convention in London. During this freedom reigns conference Mott met the more radical Stanton, who in addition to liberating slaves, had hopes of freeing turtles from their shells, and tea from the oppressive pot.

Mott and Stanton became fast friends. Once they began talking, they decided there was a laundry list of rights women should fight for. In addition to the right to vote, the dynamic duo also decided to fight for tampons in women's restrooms, sports jerseys to come in pink, and Vietnamese-owned nail salons in every strip plaza. Just as momentum seemed to be building, the Civil War came along to distract attention away from women's voting rights. Women and blacks shared the distinction of being equally unimportant when it came to selecting the president of the United States. But the passing of the fourteenth and fifteenth amendments were about to have the same effect as if women's husbands around the country told them they did indeed look fat in that dress.

Women on Bottom

Women were royally pissed in 1868, not because it was their time of the month, but at the ratification of the Fourteenth Amendment because it defined "citizenship" and "voters" as "male," and raised the question as to whether women were considered citizens of the United States at all. Then the insulting Fifteenth Amendment came along and gave black men the right to vote. The black man had successfully leapfrogged women on the rights ladder. Tempers flared among women's rights groups, and incidents of burning bras and hairy legs began to rise at an alarming rate.

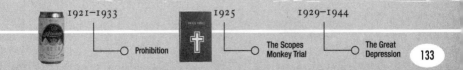

1921–1933   1925   1929–1944

Prohibition   The Scopes Monkey Trial   The Great Depression

The Holy Grail

After years of nagging, whining, foot stomping, and withholding of sexual favors, women got the right to vote as both houses of Congress passed the Nineteenth Amendment, and in 1920 it became ratified under the presidency of Woodrow Wilson. ☞ *MANY SEXIEST MEN FELT THE PASSAGE OF THE NINETEENTH AMENDMENT WAS LIKE GIVING THE CAR KEYS TO A DRUNKEN MONKEY.* ☜ Unfortunately, for the many women who decided to vote, they soon realized that even with the right to vote, super-delegates and the Electoral College still guaranteed that men would continue to get the final say on the issue of who is elected as president.

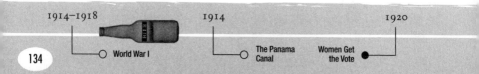

1914–1918   World War I

1914   The Panama Canal

Women Get the Vote

1920

PROHIBITION

Amendments are like blackjack

Volstead, You Are Not My Daddy

It is likely Minnesota Republican congressman Andrew Volstead's heart was in the right place when he was leading the charge for the National Prohibition Act, just not his head. The "Noble Experiment," as the Eighteenth Amendment is called, was a complete disaster—on a par with the time you suggested a threesome to your girlfriend and her best friend.

The reasons cited for enacting the Prohibition Law were to reduce crime, corruption, and poverty; solve social and morality problems; and improve the general health and hygiene of Americans. Alcohol was being blamed for everything from bad breath to violent crime. With a constitutional amendment,

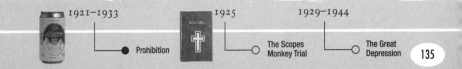

Volstead and his fellow legislators made it illegal to transport, sell, manufacture and most importantly consume alcoholic beverages.

On October 10, 1919, with a vote of 321–70, Congress put the wheels in motion for the complete prohibition of alcohol beginning January 16, 1920.

☞ *The government telling Americans they cannot drink alcohol is like a parent telling a kid he can't have a television in their room.* ✍ If the kid really wants a television they are going to whine, cry, and break the rules if needed to get it. So it was with adults in 1920 who wanted to have an alcoholic beverage; they were going to find a way to have it.

The January 15 Binge

With the complete elimination of legal consumption of alcohol the following day, you would think most Americans who enjoyed an intoxicating beverage would go on a wild drink-till-you-throw-up binger the night before. Although many people symbolically participated in "one last night" of drinking, the reality is most people just made plans to find alternatives for acquiring their alcohol.

With the convenience of buying alcohol gone but the urge for a drink remaining equal to pre–Eighteenth Amendment levels, Americans were forced to become much more creative in how they caught their next buzz. People with excess capital in their wallets were surprised at how well they got along with the underworld. Organized crime was relentless in their efforts to make sure that Americans who wanted to drink, and could afford to drink, could find a drink.

In fact, speakeasies became all the rage for those who could afford it. These private, members-only clubs where you could drink behind closed doors popped up everywhere. By some counts there were over 100,000 speakeasies in New York City alone. On the other hand, those who found their personal re-

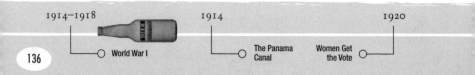

sources inadequate began creating their own home brews. They tinkered until they had some awful-tasting concoction that gave them a cheap buzz in their basement.

Drinking Can Kill You!

The good news for those who could afford to buy a drink from organized crime was that it was easily accessible. The bad news was they could get caught up in a gunfight buying it. The bootlegging industry was huge, and guys like Al Capone were enjoying the riches of supplying alcohol to the common man. Unfortunately, these high profits caused bootlegging turf wars. There were, on average, 400 murders a year related to the production and sale of alcohol in Chicago alone. Buying liquor became more than just a contact sport; it became a game of *Survivor*.

Now those who could not afford to buy booze from gangsters were not safe either. They may not share the same risk as being caught in the crossfire of rival gangs when obtaining their booze that their wealthier counterparts did. No, the risk for the poor was in home-brewed moonshine. Deaths from poisoned liquor grew from 1,064 in 1920 to 4,154 in 1925. At a glance, it is easy to reason that anytime the death rate goes up 400 percent it is never a good thing.

Twenty-One Is Better Than Eighteen

The primary reason Prohibition was a failure was lack of financial support by the federal government. Without the proper funding, enforcement became impossible. It took thirteen years of putting Americans in the awkward position of breaking the law every time they took a sip of booze before the Constitution was amended a second time with respect to alcohol.

1921–1933 — Prohibition

1925 — The Scopes Monkey Trial

1929–1944 — The Great Depression

The Eighteenth Amendment did little to improve the quality of life of Americans, and the government suffered from not being able to tax revenue associated with the production and distribution of alcohol. As a result, on December 5, 1933, just like all the parents around the country who gave in and got their kid a 46-inch wall mounted flat screen television with HBO for their bedroom, the U.S. government voted in the Twenty-first Amendment, which effectively wiped out the eighteenth, and made producing, transporting, and consuming alcoholic beverages legal again. For most Americans, the amendments are like blackjack, and twenty-one is always better than eighteen.

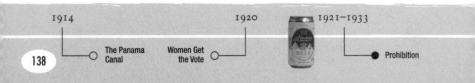

1914

The Panama
Canal

Women Get
the Vote

1920

1921–1933

Prohibition

Thankfully alcohol and the understanding of its pleasures extend outside of working America. Today Capitol Hill is full of legislators who enjoy downing a cocktail or two. For some, it is enough to have a glass of Merlot after "a health care for kids!" snubbing vote. For others, a mind-bending drink-till-you-can't-see binger helps to hide the shame of keeping sick kids from capable doctors. Unfortunately, what Barack Obama becoming the first blackish president of the United States proves is that anything really is possible.

With this in mind, ask yourself what would happen if the same religious zealots that have managed to get alcohol sales restricted on Sundays in some areas found their own Obama and he or she managed to pass a constitutional amendment forbidding the sale and consumption of alcohol, circa today? What would be the top ten drinking experiences that Americans would miss most? Here is our best guess.

1. **Fridays.** Maybe you skipped class after you shacked up with a less-than-attractive girl Thursday night, resulting in a head-down, hat-on walk of shame to get home. Or as rumors fly around the office all week about possible layoffs, you get called into your boss's office at 4:55 P.M. Friday afternoon and he tells you that as of Monday you are no longer welcome to visit the property and provides you with directions to the area's unemployment office. Not deterred, as you walk out the door for the final time, you ask the receptionist if she is interested in getting blotto and doing something (that would be you) she will undoubtedly regret later. **Recommended Beverage:** Cold, cold beer

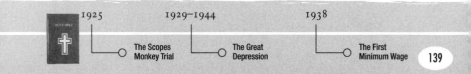

1925 — The Scopes Monkey Trial

1929–1944 — The Great Depression

1938 — The First Minimum Wage

2. **Tailgating.** What better way to rev up for the big game? For the most part, tailgating consists of overweight fans downing combo platters of wings, nachos, and brats. A special note to Anderson Cooper of CNN: if you tailgate in Austin, Texas, and get lucky, you may see Matthew McConaughey shirtless.
Recommended Beverage: Cold Beer

3. **Your 21st Birthday.** Your so-called buddies pour various shots down your throat until you puke, pass out, or become a triathlete. What could be better?
Recommended Beverage: Keep switching between various liquors and beers, with a final flaming sambuca shot to get the bile going north.

4. **New Year's Eve.** Even though it is amateur night, the overcrowded bar scene should increase the numerator of how many people are out to get laid that night. With the alcohol flowing, it is probably your best chance of the year to find noncommittal recreational sex.
Recommended Beverage: Long Island Iced Tea. After four or five of these, most members of the opposite sex will look tongue-worthy at midnight.

5. **College Graduation.** You just skated your way through a somewhat reputable four-year university, piling up enormous amounts of student loans. With scores of life experiences and a piece of paper to take with you, you realize that the likelihood of ever climbing out of debt is slim to none. Realizing that you are in for a lifetime of harassing phone calls from the collection agency that your student loan company will eventually turn your account over to, you are in the mood to celebrate.
Recommended Beverage: Bourbon and water, topped off with a few beers to finish off the evening.

6. **Happy Hour.** It's five o'clock somewhere! Round up the office posse and head to the nearby watering hole for some drinks, bad karaoke, and even worse dancing.
Recommended Beverage: Margaritas

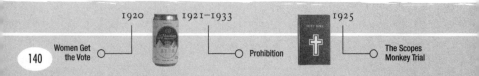

1920 — Women Get the Vote ○   1921–1933 — Prohibition ○   1925 — The Scopes Monkey Trial ○

7. **Office Party.** Where else can you get together a bunch of people with repressed feelings, both positive and negative, add liberal amounts of alcohol, and watch the drama unfold firsthand? Inappropriate hook-ups, office affairs revealed, slighted employees going off on their boss — nothing is better or more unpredictable. Not to mention the palpable level of discomfort on Monday.
   Recommended Beverage: Rum Punch and Spiked Eggnog

8. **Weddings.** The happy couple mockingly laughs at the country's 52 percent divorce rate — it won't happen to them. Not tonight at least! Whether you have known your date for five years or five minutes, it helps to have some liquid courage.
   Recommended Beverage: Pure grain alcohol if you can find it. If not, fill a flask with something that has plenty of kick.

9. **Bachelor Party.** You're sending one of your buddies off into the married world. They have found that magical someone. This alleged love of their life is someone they are willing to devote themselves to and potentially even procreate with. You superimpose an image of the couple's DNA together in your mind and wince. It's going to be a long, strange, trip.
   Recommended Beverage: Appletinis. Just kidding, unless you attended the University of Virginia. Go with top-shelf gin and tonics.

10. **Drinking in Vegas.** Even though you have to watch a handful of idiots get real loud every time they announce to the whole bar that they are doing another Jager-bomb, it is still the best place to get your drink on. What else are you to do when you are trading bad jokes with your friends while losing your shirt at the blackjack table? Pound an alcohol-free ginger ale when the dealer pulls out a 5 with 16 up? Not a chance. Liquid stupidity is part of the Vegas experience.
    Recommended Beverage: Crown and Coke, mixed in with some beers to keep the twenty-four-hour buzz going.

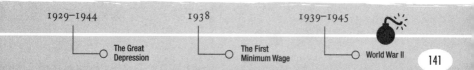

1925

THE SCOPES MONKEY TRIAL

A Matlock-esque flare for the dramatic

The Blame Game

By the mid 1920s, people all around the United States were looking for someone to blame. With millions of alcohol-loving humans suffering through the difficulties of prohibition, questions were being asked about who was ultimately responsible for the severely flawed and newly sober human race living within the borders of the continental United States. The question was kindly answered by a Tennessee court when an attention-seeking high school teacher ignored a state law that forbade the teaching of any other theory of human creation than the one that states that God created man.

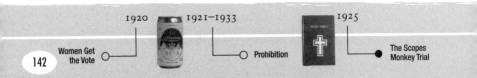

1920
Women Get
the Vote

1921–1933
Prohibition

1925
The Scopes
Monkey Trial

142

The Butler Did It

In 1925, Tennessee passed the Butler Act, which prohibited teachers in the Tennessee school system from teaching any theory of man's creation other than the one put forth in the Bible. The American Civil Liberties Union decided to get involved and set up a test case in which they would handle the defense for the guinea pig.

John "Darwin" Scopes, friend of the ape, politely raised his hand and volunteered for the job. At the behest of the ACLU, Scopes ignored the Butler Act and lectured his students that man was not created in the image of the glorious one but rather developed over time through genetic upgrades, culminating in the monkey-to-man transition.

Monkey Business

Following a Rolling Stones concert on May 5, 1925, Scopes was taken into police custody for talking too much monkey in the classroom. With his freedom on the line and fearing that the state penitentiary was full of angry, sexually suppressed men, Scopes declined to be represented by the inadequately trained and incompetent Public Defender's Office, instead electing to put his freedom in the hands of Clarence Darrow. Darrow was a noted legal scholar with a Matlock-esque flare for the dramatic. Using the moniker of the "trial of the century" as a tease, the media covered the trial gavel-to-gavel. ☞ *To cover the courtroom circus, Fox News sent a pre-facelift Greta Van Susteren, The Daily Show sent John Oliver, and Nancy Grace of CNN just screamed incessantly about Scopes's guilt.* ☜

The prosecution set out to prove that Scopes hated God, God's only son, the Holy Spirit, and even the Victoria Secret Angels. On the other hand,

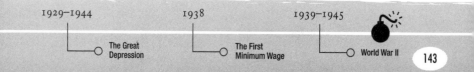

1929–1944 — The Great Depression

1938 — The First Minimum Wage

1939–1945 — World War II

Darrow argued that a strict interpretation of the Bible was impossible, as much of what the Bible contains is someone's interpretation.

Son of a Preacher Man

The judge in the case, a forefather of Lance Ito, had a constant fire in his eyes and brimstone-scented cologne on his neck. He did everything short of a change of venue to the nearest church to aid the prosecution. He chose to neglect defense arguments in favor of evolution and limited their witnesses, making it nearly impossible for the defense to convert the already guilty-leaning jury.

With strict jury instructions handed down from the judge, the jury inconvenienced themselves for an additional nine minutes to reach a decision that Scopes was guilty. Once the verdict was announced the judge quickly ordered Scopes to pay an exorbitant fine of $100. ☞ *THE VERDICT WAS LATER APPEALED, AND THE BUTLER ACT REMOVED, ALLOWING SCHOOL TEACHERS TO TALK AS MUCH MONKEY IN THE CLASSROOM AS THEY WANT.* ✌

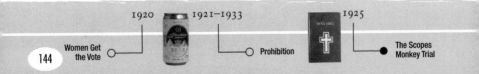

1920   1921–1933

Women Get   Prohibition
the Vote

144

1925

The Scopes
Monkey Trial

THE GREAT DEPRESSION

A Sarah Palin-at-Neiman-Marcus-like spending spree

Shop 'til You Drop

The Roaring Twenties was a period of fun and excess rivaled only by the she-nanigans of an AIG executive retreat. The federal government dictated an easy-money policy, whoring out cash to nearly anyone at obnoxiously low interest rates. This expansion of debt for the average American and the popularity of installment loans led Americans on a Sarah Palin-at-Neiman-Marcus-like spending spree. Also fueling the engine of economic disaster was the stock market's rapid progression, causing irrational exuberance. In fact, it was even popular to take the equity out of your home to invest in the can't-miss investment opportunities in the stock market. ☞ *But like new Coke, parachute pants, and* **Rocky 5**, *what seemed like a good idea at the time had unexpected consequences.* ✑

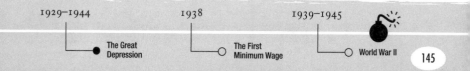

1929–1944

The Great
Depression

1938

The First
Minimum Wage

1939–1945

World War II

145

The Party's Over

By the end of these high times, the country had produced greater than its capacity to consume, and it was like Kobayashi versus Oscar Mayer. The consumers who had driven the economy sky high in the 1920s were out of credit, and restrictive overseas tariffs left the U.S. with nowhere to sell its goods. With stadiums full of goods that nobody could afford to buy, everything went on sale. Noted economist and madam to the stars Heidi Fleiss pointed out that prostitution does not have the carrying costs associated with tangible goods and therefore is a business model that more entrepreneurial woman should entertain.

With corporate profits falling like John Kerry's popularity following the airing of the Swift boat ads, companies were left with no choice but to lower their costs by politely informing many of their workers that their attendance was no longer required.

The unemployment rate went from the 3 percent who found working too inconvenient before the Depression to over 25 percent in 1933. Further complicating matters was that as unemployment climbed like a Tibetan sherpa, consumers could no longer meet their installment-payment obligations. Banks were forced to foreclose on loans. With prices falling, the repossessed goods were worth much less than the amount borrowed against them. Those who did have money realized that banks were in a precarious position with the high number of defaulting loans, so they started withdrawing their deposits. With bad loans and no deposits, banks began to fail. The federal government and the recently created Federal Reserve allowed banks to go under.

In 1930, 1,400 banks went out of business. This number continued to increase until 1933, when an amazing 4,000 more banks failed. Burned by bank closings and the loss of jobs, Americans became penny pinchers and began to save what little they could. This new commitment to savings only com-

1921–1933   1925   1929–1944

Prohibition   The Scopes Monkey Trial   The Great Depression

pounded the dire situation further. Realizing that prices were continuing to fall, Americans would wait as long as possible before making new purchases. The party that was enjoyed during the Roaring Twenties was officially over, and the hangover had begun.

Roosevelt Is Zoloft for the Great Depression

In 1932, Franklin D. Roosevelt ran on a promise of a New Deal for the American people. ☞ *With the old DEAL consisting of high unemployment, a struggling economy, and a swift kick in the balls, FDR easily won the White House.* ☜ In 1932 and 1933, he used up the entire alphabet in creating government agencies to increase spending and right the economy. The agencies helped reinforce business through government spending. Roosevelt knew that enormous federal expenditures were needed to pull America out of the Depression. Fortunately for Roosevelt, there was an Austrian-born politician named Adolf Hitler who became chancellor of Germany and was intent on taking over the world.

Realizing that nothing cures a struggling economy better than a global war, Roosevelt authorized excessive government spending on the war. Along with the spending, production doubled, and unemployment fell from 1933's 25 percent to 1.2 percent in 1944. The federal government had finally brought itself out of the Depression and emerged from the Second World War as an economic powerhouse.

1938

THE FIRST MINIMUM WAGE

Equal pay for employees with or without external genitalia

Feed These Families for Just Pennies a Day

Surprisingly, it was not underpaid immigrant landscapers that supporters of a mandated minimum wage were trying to protect, but rather scores of overly ambitious women who had developed an enormous appetite for joining their male counterparts in the ever-expanding workplace. The time-honored tradition of cooking, cleaning, and satisfying your husband's every sexual desire was on the way out. ☞ *As more and more women moved away from their traditional role of baby incubator and full-time homemaker, attention began to focus on what a fair and just wage should be.* ✍

The state of Massachusetts enacted a law that provided a wage floor for employees with or without external genitalia. This floor was the first time that any state government dictated the value of an American worker.

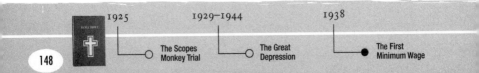

1925 — The Scopes Monkey Trial

1929–1944 — The Great Depression

1938 — The First Minimum Wage

What Are You Worth?

Over the next eleven years, fourteen more states, the District of Columbia and the, "We want to be part of the union; we don't want to be part of the union," conflicted island of Puerto Rico all jumped on the wage-mandating train. Most of the governments set up regulatory boards that ensured that the lowest allowable wage was equal to the local cost of living. For example, the wage calculation may turn out to be $0.55 an hour in Atlanta while it equals out to two tacos and a bean burrito in Puerto Rico.

How Low Can You Go?

This explosion of enthusiasm for government-backed higher wages resulted in the business community fighting back to protect their ability to pay women a discouraging low wage. They felt so strongly about the inequality of women's efforts that they began arguing their case to abandon minimum wage laws in front of the Supreme Court in 1923.

☞ Pointing to the "fact" that a white male can do the work of two women and a black man, New Jersey's finest courtroom attorney and **My Cousin Vinny** lead Vincent Gambini convinced the Supreme Court that the enforcement of wage floors was discriminatory to hard working white males. ☜ This argument proved to have some legs, as the Supreme Court struck down minimum-wage laws, and the ability to pay peasant-like wages to women quickly returned, exotic dancers being the exception.

FDR Does the Minimum

A decade and a half later, sympathizer to the poor President Franklin D. Roosevelt signed the Fair Labor Standards Act, which was a federal law that

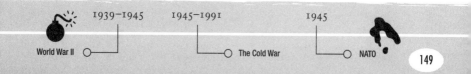

required American workers to receive a minimum of twenty-five cents an hour for their time and effort while at work. Critics claim that the minimum wage hurts small business owners, while proponents claim it helps motivate workers. But if you are cleaning up shit in a McDonald's bathroom for minimum wage, the motivation bird has probably already flown the coop. Although the federal minimum wage has been adjusted over the last several decades, Florida farmers have continued to enjoy their agricultural exemption and continue to pay the illegals picking their citrus the original twenty-five cents an hour outlined in 1938.

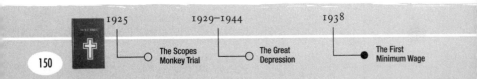

1925
The Scopes
Monkey Trial

1929–1944
The Great
Depression

1938
The First
Minimum Wage

WORLD WAR II

Mike Ricci ugly

German Uprising

In 1919, at the end of World War I, a defeated and disgruntled Germany signed the punishing treaty of Versailles. This treaty proved to be unpopular with the German government, as it limited their military, gave away large amounts of their land, and worst of all, set a curfew and limited drinking at their Oktoberfest celebrations.

In 1933, the rising German "politician" Adolf Hitler, fan of the "drink till you puke and then drink some more" routine at past Oktoberfests, found these terms unacceptable. In short, he was pissed. When the current German president died in 1934, Hitler and the Nazi Party installed themselves as the government. As soon as Hitler gained power he bailed on the Treaty of Versailles, announced he hated Jewish people, and began drafting a strong

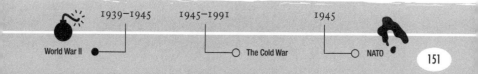

German Army via conscription. Sensing trouble, the United States quickly passed the Neutrality Act, just to let everyone know which side we were on.

All Hell Breaks Loose

At this point, global order began to break down. Mussolini's Italian forces took over Ethiopia in 1936 for their bountiful crops and easy-to-cultivate land. Proving there was something in the air, Spain orgasmically erupted into civil war that same year, and Joseph Stalin, strong-arm dictator of the Soviet Union, began a purge of resistance in his Communist house of pain.

In 1939, the Nazi's took over the unpronounceable nation of Czechoslovakia. And although there was no full-scale war, Germany and Italy signed the so-called Pact of Steel, guaranteeing both countries' leaders would take the new Cialis once a day to ensure things were rock hard when needed. Hitler followed this up by signing a nonaggression pact with Russia in 1939, effectively covering Germany's ass from being attacked on both sides.

With war now seeming more likely than not, Britain readied its armed forces on August 31, 1939. The very next day, Germany invaded Poland. Britain, France, Australia, and, thankfully, New Zealand immediately declared war on Germany. Making sure there was no confusion, the United States again publicly stated its neutrality. With the United States playing Swiss, our friendly neighbors to the north declared war on Germany on September 10, 1939. Inspired by how quickly they crushed the resistance in their own country, Russia joined Germany in double-teaming Poland, who went down like a nympho on ecstasy. Satisfied but not completely satisfied, the Soviets quickly turned and invaded Finland, as war raged on all throughout Europe.

Germany followed up its confidence-building early victory by attacking Denmark, Norway, France, and Belgium, to name a few. ☞ *LiKE HugH HEfNER dOES wiTH wOMEN, GERMANy WAS TAKiNg ON cOuNTRiES THREE AT*

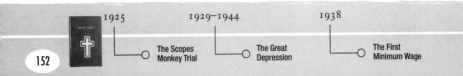

1925 — The Scopes Monkey Trial

1929–1944 — The Great Depression

1938 — The First Minimum Wage

A time. ◄ Italy, no longer hiding its red, white, and green colors, declared war on Britain and France in June 1940. Also in June the Germans took Paris, and by August, Hitler's forces began their first bombing missions of London.

The United States Takes the Plunge

By 1941, things were Mike Ricci ugly. Showing no signs of slowing down, Germany sent its first troops to Africa and began invasions in Greece and Yugoslavia. Hitler then ignored his earlier agreement with Stalin and instead invaded his vodka-appreciating country. The confused and defense-deficient Soviets quickly signed a mutual-assistance agreement with the British. In August, the United States finally dipped its toe into the water and signed the Atlantic Charter with Great Britain.

☞ *DEPENDING ON YOUR AGE, PEARL HARBOR IS EITHER YET ANOTHER MEDIOCRE BEN AFFLECK MOVIE OR ONE OF THE SCARIEST DAYS OF YOUR LIFE.* ◄ On Sunday December 7, 1941, Japanese warplanes bombed Pearl Harbor and the U.S. Naval Headquarters on the Hawaiian island of Oahu. The battlefield of World War II had spilled over onto American soil. The war was about to change.

The Tide Slowly Turns

Americans were outraged by the attack and the surprise nature of it. There was an infusion of volunteers for the U.S. military. The United States and Britain immediately declared war on Japan, and Germany, in turn, declared war on the Unites States. As the United States and Britain joined forces, the tide started to turn in favor of the Allies. By November 1942, even the Russians were starting to show some fight against the Germans.

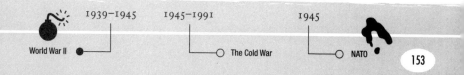

1939–1945   1945–1991   1945

World War II ●━━━┓   ┣━○ The Cold War   ┗━○ NATO

The Final Act

By 1942, German and Italian troops were surrendering in Africa. Allied troops took over Sicily. Italy, showing all of the conviction of a fat man at a dessert bar, soon surrendered to the Allies and then declared war on Germany, their former ally. On June 6, 1944, American troops needed to establish a foothold in Europe to begin their operations. After much debate, Normandy, France, was chosen as the spot of choice, despite its being well fortified by German forces.

Allied troops stormed the beaches of Normandy, where they met unthinkable resistance. Before engaging, General Eisenhower was said to give the simple but inspiring command, "Full victory—nothing else." The cost of admission into this horror flick was thousands of American lives. The beach stormers paid the price for their victory. As the plaque in the Eisenhower museum reads, "Almost 133,000 troops from England, Canada, and the United States landed on D-Day. Casualties from the three countries during the landing numbered 10,300. By June 30th, over 850,000 men, 148,000 vehicles, and 570,000 tons of supplies had landed on the Normandy shores."

By August 25, 1944, the Allies had liberated Paris as more and more allied victories became the norm. Disappointed with the direction his attempt for world domination was going, Hitler decided he couldn't win, and on April 30, 1945, he conveniently committed suicide.

As news of his timely death spread, Germans everywhere were eagerly surrendering. Despite the writing on the wall, Japan kept on fighting, and on August 6, 1945, the United States dropped the first atomic bomb on Hiroshima, Japan. As the message was not sinking in, America dropped a second atomic bomb on Nagasaki, Japan, on April 9, 1945, and Japan surrendered.

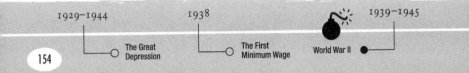

1929–1944   1938   1939–1945

The Great Depression   The First Minimum Wage   World War II

Epilogue

World War II made Germany look so bad that even giving us Heidi Klum isn't enough to make up for the damage. Hitler made good on his hate for Jewish people, as a staggering 6 million were killed in concentration camps during the war. At the end of the day, Hitler makes Osama Bin Laden look like a teenage punk with a can of spray paint. The estimates of those killed in the war are mind numbing. Germany lost approximately 8.3 million people, of which 20 percent were civilians. The Allied count was a staggering 39.9 million, with civilians making up over half that number.

The result of the war shaped the world as we know it today. The United States, Great Britain, and the Soviet Union emerged as the dominant global players. ☞ *NATO WAS FORMED, AND GERMANY EVENTUALLY BECAME KNOWN MORE FOR BEER AND SAUSAGE THAN ASPIRATIONS OF GLOBAL DOMINATION.* ☜

1945–1991   1945   1949–1954

○ The Cold War   ○ NATO   ○ McCarthyism

THE COLD WAR

1-2-3-4, I declare a thumb war

You're as Cold as Ice

Brrr! The Cold War was not the battle between Dairy Queen and Baskin Robbins to establish ice-cream supremacy and the right to feed overweight and willing Americans all the high-caloric dairy products they could ever eat. No, the Cold War entailed the competition on all fronts between the Soviet Union, the United States, and their respective allies and puppet governments. ☞ *THE COMPETITION WAS ABOUT AS SUBTLE AS A MESSAGE ON YOUR ANSWER-ing MACHINE FROM PAT O'BRIEN OR A MARV ALBERT TOUPEE.* ☜ So whether it was the arms race, the space race, or a three-legged race, the two superpowers were in competition over anything and everything.

1938 — The First Minimum Wage   World War II   1939–1945   1945–1991 — The Cold War

The Cold Shoulder

Allies at the conclusion of World War II, the United States and the USSR turned enemies as they disagreed on how to put the world back together again. Their different government philosophies made things extremely difficult. Like two giants entangled in a massive game of "1-2-3-4, I declare a thumb war," these two nations fought indirectly for the better part of four decades.

The Korean War, Vietnam War, and the Soviet-Afghan crisis were all wars in which the United States and the Soviets did battle without having an all out Hearns/Sugar Ray throw-down. Terms of endearment like "mutual assured destruction" prevented the two foes from pushing the big red button, launching nukes at each other, and throwing the world into nuclear chaos.

From the jump, the Soviets pushed for international supremacy. They defended their right to spread communism globally despite its shortcomings, while at the same time attempting to intimidate the United States. In 1957, the Soviets shot a little fear into the American mindset when they launched the first intercontinental ballistic missile and, later that same year, sent the first satellite, named Sputnik, into orbit. Four years later, in 1961, Mother Russia demanded the withdrawal of all Allied troops from Berlin, Germany. When they received a polite, yet firm "no," they created scores of day-labor jobs by building a "keep the people in" wall.

As the arms race continued, a game of chicken ensued. Both superpowers stockpiled enough nukes to blow up our planet, Venus, Mercury, and our planet again. In 1962, the Cuban Missile Crisis brought the two nations to the brink of war. Finally, cooler heads prevailed, as neither nation wanted to bring nuclear winter to the world. Tension eased slightly, and the world breathed a sigh of relief.

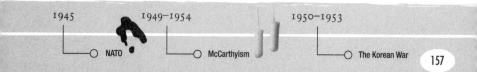

1945

1949–1954

1950–1953

NATO

McCarthyism

The Korean War

Siberian Rocky Road

As the years dragged on like an unhappy sexless marriage, the Soviet Union continued to spend gazillions of rubles on an arsenal of weapons designed to destroy the United States, to the detriment of their own people's standard of living. ☞ *Once President Reagan ran out of birthmark jokes, Soviet President Mikhail Gorbachev agreed to an arms reduction between the two nations.* ☜ This reduction was followed by the Soviet Union embracing its own version of capitalism.

Unfortunately for Gorbachev, he learned that capitalism is no quick fix for a struggling economy. After years of experimenting with capitalism, the Russian people are now enjoying the good with the bad. For many, the best part of capitalism is their new-found choices in American ice cream.

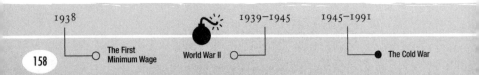

1938   The First Minimum Wage   World War II   1939–1945   1945–1991   The Cold War

1949

THE FORMATION OF NATO

A "who's who" and a "who's not" of developed and developing countries

Rhymes with Potato

Some people think the NATO acronym stands for **N**ations **A**merica **T**ea Bags **O**ften. However, a smaller, less-informed population refers to it as the North Atlantic Treaty Organization. Since 1949, this organization has operated as a military front, designed to encourage smaller, strategically located countries to willingly allow the United States and Britain access to their country's land bases and air space in exchange for protection from the unpredictable and inherently aggressive Soviet/Russian government.

The group's membership reads like a "who's who" and a "who's not" of developed and developing countries. Countries on the roster include recognizable names like Canada, France, and Germany, along with many not-so-recognizable names like Estonia, Latvia, and Slovenia. For many Americans, it

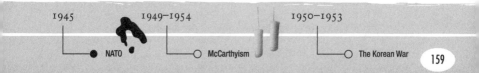

1945

1949–1954

1950–1953

NATO

McCarthyism

The Korean War

is the fact that Slovenia is contractually obligated to have our American back that allows them to sleep comfortably through the night.

The current group of twenty-six members has recently become more selective in their acceptance of new protection-seeking countries. It is believed that if the new guidelines were in place from the inception, countries with little to offer like Hungary, Iceland, and Luxembourg would currently be on the outside of the NATO window looking in.

Who's In Charge Here?

NATO defines itself as an organization that protects the freedom and security of its member countries by political and military means. This means that if a member country is feeling a little confrontational, they can confidently mouth off all they want, because if nonmember countries react aggressively toward them, it results in a series of American and British "shock and awe" retaliatory bombings. This cat-and-mouse game is popular within American military circles, as it allows U.S. forces to experiment with new and exciting toys of war on easily defeated opponents.

☞ *Much like the formula to Coke Classic and the Colonel's secret chicken recipe, the NATO hierarchy is a deep secret.* ✑ It has often been suspected that either Bulgaria is at the top of the organizational chart, because of the chaotic nature in which the organization operates, or the United States is the top monkey pulling the strings, because of how often they get their own way. There is no real evidence to disprove either theory, and ongoing smart money seems to be drifting toward a third-party candidate with a lower profile, like Portugal or the Netherlands.

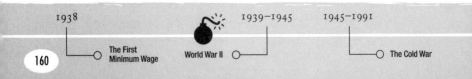

1938

The First
Minimum Wage

World War II

1939–1945

1945–1991

The Cold War

160

Getting a Little Action on the Side

Over the last several years, NATO has expanded its role to mix in a little battlefield action inside countries that are not registered to the organization but still unable to defend themselves against atrocities occurring within its borders.

In March 1999, NATO enthusiastically jumped into the Kosovo conflict, ignoring Kosovo's lack of membership. For seventy-eight days, NATO combatants enjoyed their demonstration of superiority over the in-the-wrong Serbian forces. Prior to the Kosovo involvement, NATO touched it up with the Bosnian Serb Army back in the late summer of 1995 inside Bosnia and Herzegovina. It has been rumored that there was even a French soldier who participated in the fighting before he concluded that war was beneath him and he surrendered to Serbian troops, requesting a bottle of vintage Merlot for his trouble.

Today NATO operates exactly as it was intended to. The American government gets to pick and choose which countries it would like to confront, while the rest of the membership falls in line behind them. If the West Point grads need a little mountain warfare training, the United States can influence NATO to up its involvement in Afghanistan. If snow and ice are desirable, one of the former Soviet republics offers a suitable training ground for NATO involvement. Regardless of conflict or cause, the tightly knit group of NATO members will always have America's back, because they are contractually obligated to do so—except for the second Gulf War, as nearly every one of the twenty-six countries found a loophole allowing them to forgo their military support.

To further explore the inner workings of this international military alliance, let's take a look at the FAQs from NATO'S website and interpret their evasive answers:

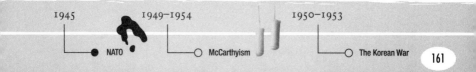

1945

1949–1954

1950–1953

NATO

McCarthyism

The Korean War

Q: What does NATO do?

A: The North Atlantic Treaty Organization (NATO) is an alliance of 26 countries from North America and Europe committed to fulfilling the goals of the North Atlantic Treaty signed on 4 April 1949. In accordance with the Treaty, the fundamental role of NATO is to safeguard the freedom and security of its member countries by political and military means. NATO is playing an increasingly important role in crisis management and peacekeeping.

Translation: NATO is a puppet organization of the United States. It currently exists to further U.S. interests in Western Europe. The United States wipes the other members' bottoms, and tucks them in at night as they suckle from our mostly prosperous capitalist teat. As the proverbial Mother Hen, the other member countries hide beneath our protective skirt when trouble comes.

Q: Does NATO have its own armed forces?

A: All member countries that participate in the military aspect of the Alliance contribute forces and equipment, which together constitute the integrated military structure of the Alliance. These forces and assets remain under national command and control until a time when they are required by NATO [for] a specific purpose (i.e. conflict or crisis, peacekeeping). NATO, however, does possess some common capabilities owned and operated by the Alliance, such as the AWACS early warning radar aircraft.

Translation: Twenty-four of the twenty-six member nations dress out some soldiers who look good in the NATO brochures. But they stay on the bench during game time. When trouble comes calling, the United States and Britain provide 99 percent of the military force. But to be fair, the organizational agenda is 99 percent provided by the United States and Britain.

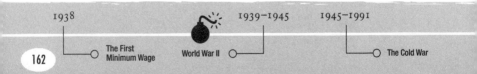

1938

162

The First
Minimum Wage

World War II

1939–1945

1945–1991

The Cold War

Q: What are the conditions for joining NATO? Which countries are eligible?

A: NATO has an open door policy with regard to enlargement. Any European country in a position to further the principles of the Washington Treaty and contribute to security in the Euro-Atlantic area can become a member of the Alliance at the invitation of the North Atlantic Council.

Countries aspiring for NATO membership are also expected to meet certain political, economic and military goals in order to ensure that they will become contributors to Alliance security as well as beneficiaries of it.

NATO's Membership Action Plan (MAP) is designed to assist aspirant partner countries in their preparations by providing a framework which enables NATO to channel assistance and practical support to them on all aspects of NATO membership.

Translation: Any country willing to put its pride on hold and bend its will to the U.S. agenda is eligible. We will protect you if you do not publicly oppose our wild and undisciplined military adventures around the world.

Q: What is NATO's position on Iraq?

A: The campaign against Iraq in 2003 was conducted by a coalition of forces from different countries, some of which were NATO member countries and some were not. NATO as an organisation had no role in the campaign but undertook a number of measures in accordance with Article 4 of the North Atlantic Treaty, to ensure the security of one of its members, Turkey, in the event of a threat to it resulting from the war in Iraq. On 21 May 2003, the Alliance also agreed to support Poland, a member of NATO, in its leadership of a sector in the stabilization force in Iraq.

In August 2004, in response to a request by the Iraqi Interim Government, NATO established a Training Implementation Mission in Iraq. NATO is involved in training, equipping, and technical assistance — not combat. The aim of the Mission is to help Iraq build the capability of its Government to address the security needs of the Iraqi people.

Translation: Look, we smelled bullshit from the start. The United States was on a wild goose chase to secure its oil interests. But we did as ordered, and did not publicly oppose them.

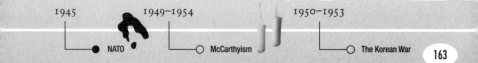

1945   1949–1954   1950–1953

NATO   McCarthyism   The Korean War

Q: What is NATO's role in the fight against terrorism?

A: On 12 September 2001, less than 24 hours after the terrorist attacks against the United States, NATO declared the attacks to be an attack against all the 19 NATO member countries within the terms of Article 5 of the North Atlantic Treaty.

This landmark decision was followed by practical measures aimed at assisting the United States in different fields, in relation to its campaign against terrorism.

Translation: We voted on Article 5 only after making sure we would not be required to do anything. Once we were given assurances it was a symbolic gesture, we couldn't rock the vote fast enough.

Q: Is NATO involved in Afghanistan?

A: Yes. Through its leadership of the International Security Assistance Force (ISAF), NATO is helping establish the conditions in which Afghanistan can enjoy a representative government and self-sustaining peace and security.

The Alliance took over command and coordination of ISAF in August 2003. Initially restricted to providing security in and around Kabul, NATO-led ISAF has gradually extended its reach and is now responsible for security across the whole country. This is the first mission outside the Euro-Atlantic area in NATO's history.

Translation: As usual, we sent a few Italians and Greeks over there to make it look good. If the United States would like to touch it up with another non-NATO country in the future we will be happy to green light their military mission.

Q: What is Russia's status — is it a partner country?

A: Yes. NATO and Russia made a reciprocal commitment to work together to build a stable, secure and undivided continent on the basis of partnership and common interest in 1997.

This commitment was strengthened in May 2002, with the establishment of the NATO-Russia Council, which brings together the 26 NATO Allies and Russia to identify and pursue opportunities for joint action at 27 as equal partners.

Translation: Of course, they are just playing along to see what our weaknesses are. They are about ten minutes from teaming up with Japan and going on the offensive.

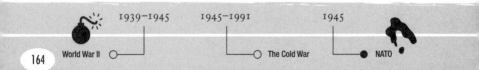

1939–1945   1945–1991   1945

World War II ○   ——————○ The Cold War   ●— NATO

Q: What are the official languages of NATO?

A: The two official languages of NATO are English and French.

> **Translation:** We had to throw the Frenchies a bone here. They are soooo high-maintenance.

Q: How much does NATO cost and who pays for it?

A: NATO is an intergovernmental organization to which member nations allocate the resources needed to enable it to function on a day-to-day basis. There are three budgets: one civil and two military. Each NATO member country pays an amount into the budgets based on an agreed cost-sharing formula. Taken together, these budgets represent less than half of one percent of the total defence budget expenditures of NATO countries.

> **Translation:** Don't believe the hype. The United States picks up the tab. More recently, we switched from prime rib to corned beef hash at NATO functions.

Q: How do I apply for a job at NATO? Who can apply?

A: Nationals of NATO member countries may apply for all posts on NATO's international staff. Appointments to most posts are made on the basis of interview panels and written tests.

> **Translation:** If you are related to a president or royalty you can probably score a cushy post that will look good on your resume while getting to backpack through Europe for a couple years.

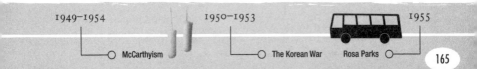

1949–1954

1950–1953

1955

McCarthyism

The Korean War

Rosa Parks

McCarthyism

Anyone with a bottle of vodka and a same-sex friend came under suspicion

What's in a Name?

There is no easy way to have your name referred to a specific act unless you truly earn it. It takes a commitment to perform an usual act that disturbs the public consciousness for your name to become a popular euphemism. For instance, if you "pull an O.J.," you killed your ex-wife and her Good Samaritan friend in a near decapitation-style murder following an unprovoked fit of rage. If you pull a Clinton, you got kinky with a cigar with an overweight intern. If you party like a Kennedy, you began drinking at 8 A.M., later driving your car off a cliff, drowning your lover, and then using your money and powerful friends to cover the whole thing up.

McCarthyism is the worst of all acts. Synonymous with promoting Communism, and generally not supporting the old U.S. of A., it has always been

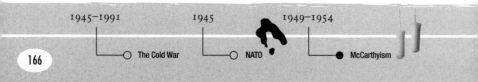

1945–1991	1945	1949–1954
The Cold War	NATO	McCarthyism

better to be a drunk, a murderer, or a lover of big women, than it is to be a proponent of Communist ideology here in America.

Red Scare Nation

Before the Red Scare of the 1940s and '50s, the most significant Red Scare for men was the monthly problem of their wife's PMS. However, during the 1940s and '50s, the Red Scare referred to Americans' fear that Communist spies were infiltrating every American organization, including the Future Polygamists of San Antonio, a high school organization.

Popular thinking was that the long-term objective of proponents for a state-run government was to hold positions of power in important organizations and then overthrow the U.S. government. Those held at the highest levels of suspicion were government employees, those in the entertainment industry, educators, and union activists. ☞ *CURRENTLY, Hollywood STARS SEAN PENN, SUSAN SARANDON, AND SHARON STONE ARE UNDER SUSPICION FOR BEHAVIOR THAT SEEMS SYMPATHETIC TO THE COMMUNIST MOVEMENT.* ☜

Red Dawn Wolverine!

In the early 1950s, a State Department official and some scientists were caught and admitted to spying and stealing secrets for the ruble-spending Soviets. Panic about the Soviets' John Holmes-ish penetration into the United States reached Jonas Brothers–level hysteria.

Looking for a little attention, Joseph McCarthy put himself in the middle of the Red Scare during a speech in February 1950. During this speech, he stated he had a list of 205 State Department employees who were Communists, along with one in six who were also either homosexual, bisexual, or bi-curious, yet still employed in the State Department shaping U.S. policy.

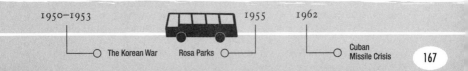

1950–1953   1955   1962

The Korean War   Rosa Parks   Cuban Missile Crisis

In 1947, the only thing worse than a gay was an aspiring gay Communist, so President Truman executed Executive Order 9835, allowing for a "loyalty review" of federal employees. If found lacking in heterosexuality or loyalty, they were fired and branded as someone who was a flag-burning America hater. It got so bad that anyone with a bottle of vodka and a same-sex friend in his house came under suspicion.

The Truman Show

Seeking and destroying possible Communist embracers did not have the support of everyone in the government. In 1950, President Truman wrote, "In a free country, we punish men for the crimes they commit, but never for the opinions they have." Later, after leaving office, he criticized the Eisenhower administration, stating, "It is now evident that the present Administration has fully embraced, for political advantage, McCarthyism. I am not referring to the Senator from Wisconsin. He is only important in that his name has taken on the dictionary meaning of the word." ☞ *Those in Wisconsin felt if Mc-Carthy truly represented them, McCarthyism would involve wearing a cheese triangle on your head while completely hammered.* ☜

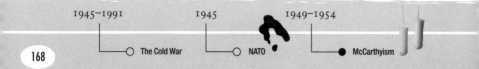

THE KOREAN WAR

A fondness for oppression

Red Angst

Five years after World War II ended and the spectacular air raids and heroic ground combat ceased, the Communist leaders of the Soviet Union were finding the day-to-day operations of a nation without free will a little tedious. They growled, and the population showed the appropriate and required amount of fear. The Communist regime gave an order, and it was followed immediately. The occasional showing of free will was squashed quickly and effectively. It was argued by many inside the police state that as enjoyable as it is to torture and maim those who share your homeland, it is always more fun to inflict fear and pain on those from other countries, especially individuals and families with an interest in open elections and freedom of choice.

Soviet president and longtime oppressor of freedom Joseph Stalin agreed with the first tenet of armed conflict, which states that even though

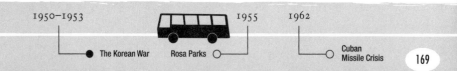

there are generally accepted issues of inconvenience when fighting a war on the road, the difficulties and expense of postwar cleanup and the reduction of the host country's civil population through friendly fire and enemy aggression far outweigh the logistical issues of traveling. In order to prove his theory, Stalin sent freedom killers from the Central Red Army to help keep peace in Korea by patrolling the area north of the thirty-eighth parallel until a unified and free, count-every-ballot election could be held in the small Asian country.

Unfortunately for those making their home in the northern part of Korea, the Soviet government had no real intention of allowing them to hold up their Iraqi like purple ink–stained thumb as proof of their participation in the democratic process. Instead, the Central Red Army was ordered to ensure that voting did not take place north of the thirty-eighth parallel. With scores of Korean citizens south of the thirty-eighth parallel earning a purple thumb on May 10, 1948, the election was deemed legitimate, and Syngman Rhee became president of the Republic of Korea, which consisted of only the land and citizens south of the thirty-eighth parallel.

Communist Masters

Left out of the democratic process by their unwelcome foreign oppressors, the area north of the thirty-eighth parallel was renamed the Democratic People's Republic of Korea, as Kim Il-sung, a Korean national who earned his master's degree in communism from the University of Phoenix's Moscow campus, was conveniently elected president without the troublesome inconvenience of a public election. President Kim had a strong mandate from the electorate, and he made plans to spread his fondness for oppression by invading those enjoying their freedom south of the thirty-eighth parallel.

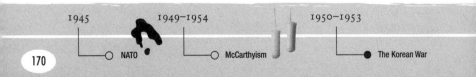

1945   1949–1954   1950–1953

○ NATO   ○ McCarthyism   ● The Korean War

On June 25, 1950, Kim ordered the North Korean People's Army to invade the Republic of Korea, killing everything in sight, while at the same time leaving behind pamphlets of the benefits of communism for the families of the dead to enjoy.

WW 2.5 Limited Edition

While mindful of the possibility of World War III breaking out over the differences in political ideology, U.S. President Harry S. Truman sent General Douglas MacArthur to defend the sovereignty of the Republic of Korea by heading up the United Nations coalition of the willing. With a U.N. mandate to unify Korea, MacArthur raised hell on both sides of the thirty-eighth parallel, forcing the North Korean Army to retreat far into the northern area of their country.

Chinese Insurgents

Progress was steady, and with victory on the horizon, MacArthur ordered a large "Mission Accomplished" banner to be displayed outside the Korean National Zoo. As those fighting against the spread of communism began to make plans to enjoy the spoils of their victory with thankful Korean woman, 180,000 communist sympathizers from China entered the war in support of Kim.

Using the strength in numbers approach, the 180,000 oppression spreaders overwhelmed U.N. forces, forcing many of them back into the southern portion of Korea. With China now fully involved in the war, MacArthur urged Truman to allow him to attack China as retaliation for their intervention. Fearing all-out nuclear war, Truman ordered MacArthur to focus on fighting the war on Korean turf and ignore his desire to tangle with China on their soil.

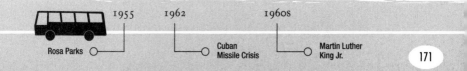

1955   1962   1960s

Rosa Parks

Cuban Missile Crisis

Martin Luther King Jr.

With the North Koreans, the Chinese, and the Soviets all heavily involved in the fight for this small, moderately priced guitar-producing nation, the coalition of the willing slowly was becoming the coalition of the less than willing. As their desire to take on China diminished, enthusiasm for a cease-fire was growing.

With millions dead and the postwar cleanup significant, the war ended on July 27, 1953. Leaning on their newly established relationship with the active human breeders in China, the country of North Korea began to use state-approved Chinese breeding techniques to replenish their postwar population.

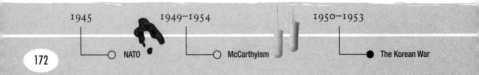

1945

1949–1954

1950–1953

NATO

McCarthyism

The Korean War

ROSA PARKS

Huge fan of public transportation

Move to the Black of the Bus

When Rosa Parks her ass on a bus, people listen. As a part-time car enthusiast and a full-time realist, Parks knew the wages paid to her as a black woman would never afford her the opportunity to drive the car of her dreams, a converted Crown Victoria cop car pimped out with twenty-two-inch rims and aftermarket hydraulics. Instead, leaning on her penchant for reality, Parks became a huge fan of public transportation. There was no three-wheel motion, no rims, and no stereo, but at least it got you from one miserable destination to another in a not-so-timely manner.

Parks rode her transportation vehicle of affordable choice without incident until December 1, 1955, when she got a hair up her ass concerning the Jim Crow laws of separate and unequal. These laws were designed to allow black and white people to live in perfect harmony like ebony and ivory or Michael

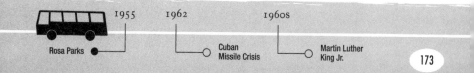

1955   1962   1960s

Rosa Parks

Cuban
Missile Crisis

Martin Luther
King Jr.

173

Jackson's DNA, providing blacks were submissive to the desires of God's Caucasian people. The public transportation system was a great opportunity for African Americans to demonstrate their required submissiveness by willingly and happily sitting at the back of the bus. It was expected that black people would eagerly give up their seat so white men and woman could rest their tired, pale legs if the bus became crowded. There was an understanding and sympathy about the burden of being white in a white society by the minority bus-riding population.

As the bus made its rounds on that fateful December day, more and more of America's majority boarded Rosa's bus of choice. As the driver continued to move the "colored section" sign farther back in the bus to accommodate the additional white passengers, Rosa stayed put. When the driver threatened to call the police, Rosa told him to go for it. As the police officer arrested Rosa, she thanked the bus driver for his racially biased actions.

More Empty Seats than New Yankee Stadium

Capitalizing on Rosa's arrest, Montgomery, Alabama, pastor and aspiring civil rights leader Martin Luther King headed up a boycott of the local public transportation system. On December 5, 1955, nearly 90 percent of all the black people who had complacently been sitting at the back of the bus followed King's request and surprisingly found another way to travel to their destination. ☞ *With the overwhelming support he received on day one of the boycott, King pushed for a second day, then a week, then a month, and then a year. King's peaceful protests attracted national coverage, culminating with a fair and balanced interview on the* **O'Reilly Factor**. ☜

As lawsuits were filed, the case went all the way to the U.S. Supreme Court. The Court ruled on December 20, 1956, that the segregation was illegal, im-

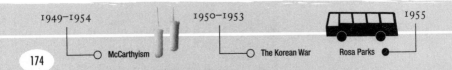

1949–1954   1950–1953   1955

○ McCarthyism   ○ The Korean War   Rosa Parks ●

mediately opening up great seats right up front next to the driver for African Americans all across the country. Unable to change the reality that she would never be able to afford her pimped out Crown Victoria that she so desperately desired because as a black woman she would always be paid less than her white counterparts, the Supreme Court also ordered that, for her trouble, Rosa Parks receive a lifetime public transportation pass allowing her to ride any bus anytime anywhere in America for free ... providing seats are available.

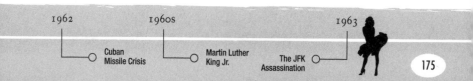

1962

Cuban Missile Crisis

Check, bet, or fold

Nuclear Chicken

In between trolling for willing and eager one-night companions within the White House secretary pool, President John F. Kennedy worked in a little game of nuclear chicken with the sometimes-sober leader of the Soviet Union, Nikita Khrushchev.

Prior to JFK placing his nonmasturbatory hand on the Bible and taking the oath of office, previous president Dwight D. Eisenhower was credited with kicking off the testosterone-filled showdown in 1959, when he deployed U.S.-made Jupiter missiles uncomfortably close to the Soviet Union border. Using the accommodating countries of Turkey and Italy to act as storage units for his toys, Eisenhower announced the purpose of the missiles was to promote peace in the region. ☞ *Upon taking office, JFK argued passionately*

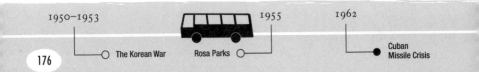

1950–1953

1955

1962

The Korean War   Rosa Parks

Cuban Missile Crisis

that the path to peace was through intercontinental extramarital affairs. ✏

He told the White House press corps that he had his eye on an insanely hot blonde from Moscow named Natasha Breastinov that he noticed while surfing the erotic services section of a popular underground Soviet website.

Nuclear Breastinov Implants

In October 1962 during negotiations, Khrushchev officially took sex with Miss Breastinov off the table and instead began building nuclear missile sites in the not-so-American-friendly and uncomfortably close nation of Cuba. President JFK was so angered by Khrushchev's unwillingness to order Miss Breastinov to have freakish sex with him in an effort to promote world peace, that he immediately blocked Khrushchev from his Facebook page. After it was discovered that Khrushchev was computer illiterate, effectively making the punishment ineffective, JFK called a meeting with Secretary of Defense Robert McNamara, at which time McNamara gave the president the same three options all gamblers face: check, bet, or fold.

Let's Make a Deal

Following an episode of the animated hit series *The Simpsons*, President Kennedy spoke to the nation about the desperate situation in a live televised address on October 22, 1962. With nuclear war a very real possibility, he assured the American people that he had done everything he could to work with Khrushchev diplomatically, even proposing that Khrushchev could have his way with Hollywood's semiostracized actress Shannen Doherty in an attempt to solve the growing crisis at hand.

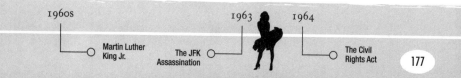

Leaning on his team of advisors and yes-men, JFK decided against attacking Russia's Cuban installations for fear of initiating an all-out nuclear war that could lead to the deaths of millions, including hundreds of yet-to-be-enjoyed Russian beauties. Instead, JFK opted for a more passive-aggressive approach by ordering a quarantine of Soviet ships trying to enter the small cigar-making island.

After several days, Khrushchev blinked and agreed to dismantle his nuclear launch sites under United Nations supervision in exchange for the United States removing its weapons from Turkey and agreeing to allow Cuban dictator Fidel Castro to carry on his dictating without fear of another U.S. attack. Having narrowly avoided a nuclear war, JFK announced that he was looking for two willing White House secretaries with Russian heritage to participate in a celebratory threesome inside the oval office.

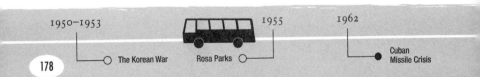

1950–1953

1955

1962

The Korean War

Rosa Parks

Cuban Missile Crisis

1960s

Martin Luther King Jr.

...things started to unravel

A Black Man's Wet Dream

Martin Luther King Jr. may have been a black man, but he shared the same sexual fantasies as most of his Caucasian male counterparts. To prove it, in June 1963 he organized a rally of 250,000 people on the steps of the Lincoln Memorial in Washington, D.C. to let Americans of all colors know publicly and emphatically that he too wanted to sleep with the hungry and emaciated Olsen twins. King told his audience that it would be an appropriate gesture of goodwill on the part of the twins if they joined him in a post civil rights rally threesome as repayment for the years of slavery that his relatives of generations past suffered through.

Using his announcement for twin-on-King love as a springboard to discuss civil rights in America, MLK Jr. spoke passionately about the need to find racial equality in the United States. He advocated for Gandhi-like power

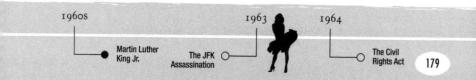

through peaceful demonstrations when he wasn't chasing down young former child star actresses.

Fortunately for King, his pleas for equality landed on the sympathetic ears of President John F. Kennedy. Kennedy openly championed the effort to bring social reform in the way of racial equality. For years, JFK carried around a list of names with corresponding pictures in his back left pocket of the black women he would like to sleep with once the social stigma of interracial relations was removed.

Keep Dreaming

MLK was on a roll. The president wanted to advance the cause of the black man, and he had the attention of African Americans everywhere.

But as his people's mojo got working, things started to unravel. JFK was assassinated during a re-election campaign stop in Dallas, Texas. The Civil Rights Act was sympathetically passed, only to have the Vietnam War take center stage. King openly rejected the war, advocating that the money being spent to fight communism in the tiny Asian country should be spent at home as an economic stimulus package for the poor.

Nightmare Scenario

In March 1968 MLK rolled into Memphis, Tennessee, to support area sanitation workers who were striking to correct the shitty treatment they had been receiving. James Earl Ray, Olsen stalker and part-time vegan, shot King dead while he stood outside on the second-floor balcony of the less-than-classy Lorraine Motel. With King's premature death, and for the good of race relations in America, Mary Kate and Ashley are now being asked to make sexual reparations with the less popular and far less attractive Reverend Al Sharpton.

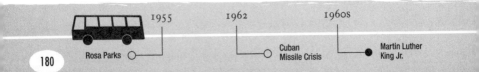

1955 — Rosa Parks
1962 — Cuban Missile Crisis
1960s — Martin Luther King Jr.

THE JFK ASSASSINATION

An appreciation for Hollywood ass

The Kennedy Presidency

Young, good-looking, and owner of the kind of power most men only dream of, JFK was our thirty-fifth president and our favorite gigolo. He was a Harvard graduate. He was an adulterer. He had an appreciation for the arts. He had an appreciation for Hollywood ass. He oftentimes invited the brightest and most creative minds to the White House. He oftentimes invited women other than his wife for sex at the White House.

He was a visionary who hoped to accomplish a number of social reforms. He was a visionary who enjoyed a quality threesome when his schedule allowed for it. During his inaugural speech he issued the famous line, "Ask not what your country can do for you, ask what you can do for your country." Behind closed doors, he issued the famous words, "Let this be our dirty little secret."

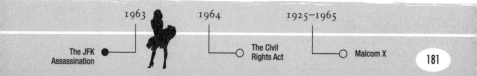

Although Kennedy enjoyed successes politically with cleaning up the growing problem of organized crime in America, and sexually with his conquests of Marilyn Monroe and Judith Campbell Exner, there were some hiccups during his presidency. Kennedy okayed the Bay of Pigs disaster and had difficulty passing social reform. In spite of his uneven first-term results, he was beginning to look toward securing re-election when he traveled to Texas in November 1963.

The Dallas Disaster

Maybe if Kennedy had been less focused on changing Washington's nickname to the "unbuckled beltway," he would have realized that sitting in the back of a convertible with the top down waving to a crowd of strangers is never a good idea for anyone who has made an enemy or two over the years. It takes only one bad day for a psychotic, socially disturbed malcontent to bring a gun to work.

As the presidential motorcade made its way through Dallas, cheering crowds lined the streets. When the president's car pulled in front of the Texas School Book Depository, three shots were fired, and chaos erupted. The first shot was wide right, the second nonfatal shot was buried deep in the spleen of the Texas governor, and the third was a fatal headshot to President John Fitzgerald Kennedy. With the president dead, police arrested Lee Harvey Oswald, the aforementioned psychotic, socially disturbed malcontent.

Who Is Responsible?

Many Americans never wanted to believe that Oswald acted on his own. As a result, dozens of theories concerning who was responsible for JFK's murder have been offered up. The Russians did it. The Mafia did it. The vice president

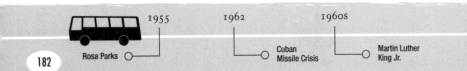

was power hungry. Who would shoot the man whose secret service detail gave the code name The Golden Penis?

Speculation ran on endlessly like a Kenyan. It was three shooters; it was a shooter on the overpass. It was a shooter on the grassy knoll. Nobody knows for sure. But most evidence leads us to believe it was Lee Harvey Oswald. Unfortunately, we never got to hear from Oswald. ☞ *As he was being transferred between prisons, strip-club owner Jack Ruby shot Oswald to death on live TV, which is a good lesson for anyone thinking about establishing credit at a strip club.* 🖎 Ruby was later arrested, tried, and sent to prison; he died from cancer in 1967.

For many Americans, the Kennedy assassination is the crown jewel of unsolved mysteries. To date there have been over 2,000 books written on the Kennedy assassination, and not one of them unequivocally holds the nuts to the question, who shot President Kennedy?

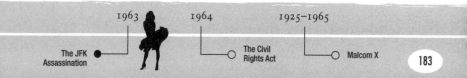

1963 — The JFK Assassination

1964 — The Civil Rights Act

1925–1965 — Malcom X

ADULTERY: A PRESIDENTIAL TRADITION

Obviously, other presidents before and after JFK have indulged in extramarital affairs; however, this is an appropriate place to pause and reflect on the all-time greatest White House mistresses, because no one did it better than John Fitzgerald Kennedy. The following rankings are based on the mistresses' looks, stature in the community, and length of sexual service to the president. There is no weight given to their skills between the sheets, as most often the presidents themselves have yet to comment on the individual performances of their mistresses.

Top Ten All-Time White House Mistresses

1. **Marilyn Monroe:** She's in a league of her own. An object of men's fantasies around the world in her prime. Even JFK's wife gave him props on this.

2. **Sally Hemings:** Sally was Thomas Jefferson's slave with whom he had children. He loved to tell her, "I own you!" because legally, he really did.

3. **Blaze Starr:** JFK scores again. She was a stripper, and frequently referred to her bedroom as the "Oral Office."

4. **Mary Gibbons:** George Washington got the presidential ball rolling with this spicy little number. It is a little-known fact that when George was talking about cutting down the cherry tree, he was actually referring to taking Mary's virginity.

5. **Judith Exner Campbell:** JFK makes his third appearance on our list. Campbell was known to be a mistress of the Chicago mobster Sam Giancana. Really JFK? We're disappointed. Sloppy seconds? C'mon! You bagged Monroe! Dust yourself off and get back out there.

1962

Cuban
Missile Crisis

1960s

Martin Luther
King Jr.

1963

The JFK
Assassination

6. **Crown Princess Marta:** Franklin Delano Roosevelt makes our list. She was the crown princess from Norway. And more importantly, she was hot.

7. **Nan Britton:** Warren Harding shows up in the #7 spot. One of the favorites on the list, Harding was president during the Roaring Twenties and bagged Britton, thirty years his junior. Harding is often described as a "compulsive adulterer."

8. **Monica Lewinsky:** Our most recent addition to the list is known for seedy encounters with President Clinton. Literally helped redefine the word sex. Now making a living off her sexual exploits.

9. **Kay Summersby:** Dwight Eisenhower's mistress during his time as a general. Some sources report it as an illicit affair, while others maintain it didn't go beyond kissing. Which one is it? We need to know. If it was only kissing, then she's off the list, and she won't have a second crack at it either. Not because we're bastards; she died in 1975.

10. **Kennedy's secretaries:** Now that's how you bounce back from sloppy seconds. A good old-fashioned threesome in the White House pool with employees. Man, this guy pulled in some serious tail. You are a role model for all American men, Mr. Kennedy.

1964

THE CIVIL RIGHTS ACT

A call-the-doctor itch for equality

Equal in War, Equal in Peace

With the sequel to the Great War over and the Korean conflict fading in the rearview mirror, black American men began to develop a call-the-doctor itch for equality. After Harry S. Truman ordered the integration of the United States military in 1947, black men were given the opportunity to live, work, and die with the more popular and more highly regarded white man.

Witnessing the ease in which a white man could get a table at a restaurant, tickets to a ball game, and purchase a car, men with African heritage took an interest in the benefits of the white man's lifestyle. Using the momentum developed by the Supreme Court ruling of 1954 calling for desegregation of U.S. public schools, black people across the United States took up the tussle for minority equality.

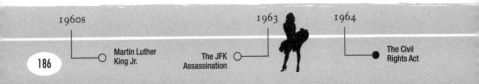

1960s — Martin Luther King Jr.

1963 — The JFK Assassination

1964 — The Civil Rights Act

Politely Asking for Equality

Instead of using the threat of death that gun-in-hand armed Robin Hoods use today to influence convenience store workers to politely and quickly put the day's revenue in a brown bag and graciously give it to them, African Americans in the earlier sixties began a much quieter movement centered on peaceful marches. Tens of thousands and at times hundreds of thousands of black people would congregate in political epicenters to kindly ask for the same opportunities that the American majority were experiencing.

Leading the way was a charismatic brutha named Martin Luther King. King met great resistance for his cause from the Confederate flag–worshipping southern males. It was obvious that King and his movement had a chance to become more than just a nuisance, threatening a real possibility of long lines at newly ordained mixed-race water fountains all around the country. ☞ *FEARing this outcome, deer-hunting, tobacco-chewing, Busch Light–drinking rednecks put forth the theological proposition that God never intended to create all men equally.* ☜

Progress Has Its Price

Unfortunately for the white southerners, the attempt to equalize the races had the support of gigolo John, the thirty-fifth president of the United States. Many people hypothesized that JFK truly cared about the equality of African Americans. Others felt that he had yet to score with a woman of color and was simply using his presidential influence to equalize the rights of minorities in order to win the favor of black women. Although anxious to see the passage of a Civil Rights Act to boost his luck with black women, JFK never realized his dream, as former New Orleans resident and self-proclaimed Marxist Lee Harvey Oswald shot him dead in Dallas, Texas.

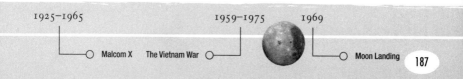

With the president dead, former vice president turned president Lyndon B. Johnson capitalized on the sympathies of legislators in the House and Senate to push through the Civil Rights Act of 1964 as a final tribute to JFK's wishes of equalizing the rights of minority Americans. Subsequently, tables at restaurants and tickets to ball games became increasingly more difficult to get with the added competition of hungry African American sports fans across the country.

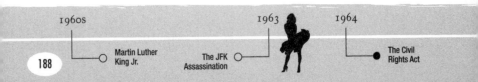

1960s

Martin Luther
King Jr.

1963

The JFK
Assassination

1964

The Civil
Rights Act

MALCOLM X

One bad-ass non-Caucasian

Who Was Malcolm X?

Malcolm was one bad-ass non-Caucasian. Born in Omaha, Nebraska, on May 19, 1925, Malcolm was Earl and Louise Little's bundle of joy. Malcolm's father was a Baptist minister who had developed a nonsexual crush on Black Nationalist leader Marcus Garvey. The man who caught Earl's platonic eye headed up the Universal Negro Improvement Association, a national organization focused on parlaying blacks' favored wartime draft status into an improved draft status for African Americans in the National Basketball Association, along with civil rights for those not talented enough to play basketball at the highest level.

Fueling Earl's passion for equality was his mistrust of the white man. At the time of Malcolm's birth, three of Earl's brothers had already met an untimely death, including a Southern-style lynching at the suspected hands of

the American majority. On a personal level, Earl also experienced a number of death threats that caused Louise and him to relocate the Little family several times.

While Malcolm was still a young child, his father met his own untimely death when he was hit by a streetcar named Ivory. Fortunately for the black community, the police reported that when they arrived at the scene Earl was conscious enough to tell them he had clumsily slipped and fell underneath the streetcar's wheel all on his own. He told the police to make sure everyone knew that no white man was involved in his death and that he apologized for any inconvenience his self-inflicted, yet accidental death would cause. Even with Earl's attempt to head off any issues, many people in the black community suspected that a white supremacist group called Black Legion was responsible for his death.

Studious X

With Malcolm's father suffering the same fate as three of his brothers and his mother earning residency at a mental hospital, Malcolm spent the next several years being passed around like a joint at a high school party as he went from foster home to foster home. Despite his difficult upbringing, he excelled academically and finished at the top of his class in junior high. Benefiting from a chance career counseling session with one of his favorite teachers, he was famously told by his "white is better" educator that his goal of becoming a lawyer was "no realistic goal for a nigger."

Malcolm quickly embraced the wise advice he received and lost interest in school. With the inconvenience of school out of his life, Malcolm began an apprenticeship in narcotics, gambling, and prostitution. Unfortunately for Malcolm, before he could complete his studies he was convicted of burglary charges in Boston and sentenced to ten years in prison.

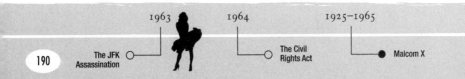

1963 — The JFK Assassination

1964 ◦— The Civil Rights Act

1925–1965 ●— Malcom X

While incarcerated, Malcolm read like a man with nothing to do. During his imprisonment, his brother Reginald would visit and discuss his conversion to the Muslim religion. Malcolm quickly became drawn to the teachings of the Nation of Islam leader Elijah Muhammad. Elijah M. had very little love for those who were not black and advocated that black people should have their own nation uninhabited by white people and polar bears. Paroled in 1952, Malcolm dropped his surname, Little, in favor of X in an effort to represent his lost tribal name as well as to intimidate white people. With an intimidating name and black power on his mind Malcolm prepared to fight the civil rights fight.

X Marks the Spot for Controversy

Malcolm's charisma and message drew frustrated African Americans to him as his reputation grew across the country as a radical civil rights leader. His outspoken nature and strong words led to government surveillance. On April 3, 1964, Malcolm gave his most famous speech, "The Ballot or the Bullet" in a church in Cleveland, Ohio. The speech centered on Malcolm X imploring African Americans to exercise their right to vote and to realize that those whom they had voted for in the past had not taken care of them.

The "Bullet" part of the speech was a message to blacks that if they were not given the equality they deserved, they should take up arms and fight for the rights promised to them as Americans. Malcolm X's support of violence turned full circle when he fell victim to sixteen bullets during a meeting of the Organization of Afro-American Unity. Three members of the Nation of Islam were later convicted of his murder.

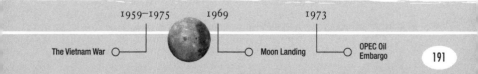

1959–1975   1969   1973

The Vietnam War   Moon Landing   OPEC Oil Embargo

THE VIETNAM WAR

Ideal for those interested in fighting in the most hellish possible places

Soldier On

Nothing rips this country apart at the seams more dramatically than an unpopular war. The idea of sending young Americans abroad to fight the fight for a country whose citizens are so geographically challenged that even the brightest of the bright couldn't find the United States on a well-labeled wall map is reason enough to piss a lot of people off. The tiny Asian country of Vietnam was one of these countries that proved to be so geographically deficient about the United States that it quickly divided our country into pro, no-pro war corners.

As for the U.S. citizens fortunate enough to enjoy a government sponsored adventure vacation to the jungles of Vietnam, their knowledge of their travel destination was limited to the handful of times they had dined on the country's cuisine.

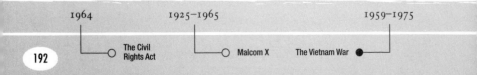

Winner, Winner, Chicken Dinner

As the war in Vietnam escalated, the Bureau of Travel and Military Affairs began to fall behind on its supply of travelers willing to make the trek to the small, impoverished country. To rectify the situation, the B.T.M.A. set up a national lottery beginning in December 1969 for giving away thousands upon thousands of vacation packages to the Asian hotspot. Unfortunately for women and the elderly, the rules of the lottery prohibited them from winning. In fact, preferential treatment was given to males aged eighteen to twenty-six.

With ticket sales sluggish but the commitment still needing to be honored, scores of young men began to receive notification in the mail of their winning lottery number, even though they couldn't recall purchasing a ticket. In addition, the trip winners received new titles like "private" and "soldier."

Meet Charlie

The U.S. soldiers, who were fortunate enough to have the government make third-class travel arrangements for them, enjoyed jungles that provided malaria, dysentery, 120-degree temperatures, 95 percent humidity, and obnoxiously inconvenient elephant grass. These conditions proved to be ideal for those interested in fighting in the most hellish possible places.

The U.S. troops were thrown into a situation where they were facing an enemy who had been waging war for many years, with a willingness to continue for years to come. The North Vietnamese guerilla-style war seemed endless because, in fact, it was. With a per-capita income of less than a dollar a day, there wasn't much for the Vietnamese to look forward to once the war concluded.

1969   1973   1972–1973

Moon Landing   OPEC Oil Embargo   Watergate

Was It 1975 or 2008?

As the war waged on with mostly reluctant lottery winners, the political battle back home waged on in the safe confines of Washington, D.C. President Kennedy, the gigolo in chief, saw the war as an opportunity to stop the spread of communism and re-establish the might of the U.S. military in the eyes of the world. ☞ *However, upon Kennedy's assassination, Lyndon B. Johnson took office and listed Vietnam as priority number 3,747—well behind establishing a division I college football playoff and determining if saline breast implants are safer then silicone implants.* ☜ As more and more Americans became frustrated with the lack of success and purpose with the war in Vietnam, LBJ's popularity began to sink. Johnson, sensing his own unpopularity, announced he was not going to run for re-election.

When You Withdraw Before Completion, Nobody Wins

With Johnson out and Tricky Dick Nixon in, the bitter and unsatisfactory end to the conflict concluded in 1975 with the total pullout of American troops. ☞ *For a handful of diehard war fans, the withdrawal was much like the pullout method for birth control—early, ineffective, and unsatisfactory.* ☜

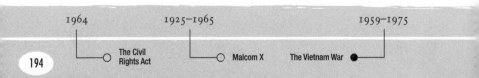

1964   1925–1965   1959–1975

The Civil Rights Act   Malcom X   The Vietnam War

1969

Moon Landing

A race between passive science geeks from each country

Anything You Can Do I Can Do Better

In 1969, love children and free love may have been the rage in the United States, but there was no love between the United States and the U.S.S.R. Our hatred for each other ran so deep that Catholic priests from Massachusetts even refused to have sex with Russian altar boys. Unable to declare a winner in the nuclear arms race, both countries turned their attention to the space race.

This race was between the more passive science geeks from each country to see who had the biggest pocket protector and least chance of getting laid. Winner takes all, if you call a celibate lifestyle a prize. Surprisingly, these scientists proved to be the ultimate wingmen, as their hard work has been getting astronauts laid for more than forty years.

The space race officially commenced on October 4, 1957, when the Soviet Union launched a thirty-eight-pound bottle of vodka named Sputnik I into

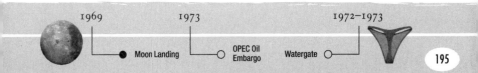

orbit. Behind and upset, President Dwight Eisenhower mercilessly flogged our geek squad until the United States launched Explorer I into orbit in January 1958.

With the space race tied up, the Russian government threatened to reassign their team of space race scientists to the salt mines of Siberia. Fearing their inability to handle the harsh outdoor conditions facing them in Siberia, the chain-smoking, Smirnoff-chugging science geeks from Russia managed to pull ahead despite their vices, and trump the Americans' effort by launching cosmonaut Yuri Gagarin into orbit in 1961. Knowing we were behind, but feeling confident because he had just slept with Marilyn Monroe, President John F. Kennedy calmly yawned and publicly announced he was sending American astronauts to land on the moon.

Redefining the Ultimate Road Trip

Over the next eight years, the U.S. government spent $45,571,162 of taxpayer money to send three overeager nerds disguised as astronauts on the ultimate road trip. ☞ *Armed with a couple of cases of beer and a box of eight-tracks, Neil Armstrong, Edwin "Buzz" Aldrin, and Michael Collins set out on the craziest, most dangerous road trip of their time.* ☜

On July 20, 1969, Armstrong and Aldrin moved their way into the lunar excursion module, separated from the command capsule, and landed safely on the moon at 4:17 P.M., Eastern Daylight Time. Realizing the first one to step onto the moon's surface would benefit from huge amounts of fame and the ability to get laid anywhere, anytime, by practically anyone on planet Earth, Armstrong pushed Aldrin to the side and made his way out of the module and onto the moon's surface.

Shortly after Armstrong, mumbled the now-famous words, "That's one small step for man and one giant leap for mankind," Aldrin stepped onto the

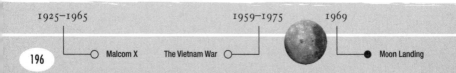

moon's surface to create his own story for the ladies. ☞ *With unbelievable bragging rights secured, they then spent the next twenty-one hours and thirty-six minutes posing for photos in front of local landmarks, partaking in regional culinary offerings, and generally immersing themselves in Moon culture.* ☜

The Results Are In

So what did Americans get for our $45,571,162?

Not much, actually. Like that one last drink you need to have at the end of a bender, it seemed really important at the time, but the expense soon became regrettable. We got forty-six pounds of moon rocks, a few hours of compelling TV, and a decent movie out of it.

The Soviets, on the other hand, were the bigger losers. Our triumphant moon landing was the first in a series of events that redefined Russian culture. After the loss of the space race, the arms race, the Cold War, and the well-publicized fight between Ivan Drago and Rocky Balboa, the Russians finally joined us in democracy. As other emerging democracies have found out, the price of freedom now includes expensive liquor and cigarettes and a struggling economy. With high unemployment and national pride at a low, Russian men are finding that passive American scientists are a threat again as they marry scores of hot Russian woman via the Internet.

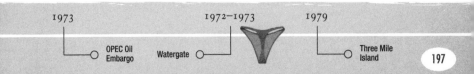

1973

1972–1973   1979

OPEC Oil
Embargo   Watergate

Three Mile
Island

1973

OPEC Oil Embargo

Buying gas was cheaper than scoring a sheet of acid

Size Does Matter

In the early 1970s, both American bong makers and American automobile buyers agreed that bigger was better. With the growing popularity of mind altering drugs in the 1970s, pot was not only plentiful it was socially acceptable. With supply high and enforcement sporadic, there was no reason for hippies of the me generation to forego an extra large bong to help them burn the cannabis. ☞ *By the same token, with gas reasonably priced, there was no need for Americans to endure the uncomfortable ride of a small car when the big three U.S. automobile manufacturers were eagerly building cars large enough to transport the real-life cast of* **Jon + Kate Plus 8.** ☜

During this time of discos and swinger parties, Americans gave more thought to the cost of condoms than they did the cost of gasoline. Buying

1959–1975   1969   1973

The Vietnam War   ○   ○ Moon Landing   ● OPEC Oil
                                                          Embargo

gas was cheaper than scoring a sheet of acid picturing John, Paul, George, and Ringo wearing Sargeant Pepper suits. Unfortunately, this cheap petroleum fest came to an end on October 17, 1973, when the Organization of Petroleum Exporting Countries refused to pimp their fuel to the United States in retaliation for its increasingly active support of Israel.

Earlier in the month, on October 7, 1973, Syria and Egypt began hostile military action as it attacked the holocaust-recovering country of Israel. This armed conflict was quickly coined the Yom Kippur War. The Israelis enjoyed very little popularity in the Middle East, and the attacks by Syria and Egypt were widely supported by Arab leaders. On the other hand the United States government has always had a fetish for Israel, and it moved to support the Israeli government by resupplying the Israeli armed forces. America's supporting of Israel like a push-up bra helped further the hatred for America in the Middle East.

Oil: America's Drug of Choice

With America's support in the open, on October 16, 1973, the Arab constituents of OPEC cut oil production, placed an embargo on exporting to the United States along with any other country aiding the Israeli war effort, and significantly raised the price of oil. This show of power was the first time that the oil-rich countries of the Middle East collectively showed their Hogan-like strength and their importance to the lifestyle of Americans. With only 6 percent of the world's population and a third of global oil consumption, the effects of the embargo were felt immediately in the United States.

With gasoline in short supply, the United States government focused on reducing consumption and rationing supply. Speed limits on highways were reduced to the cruising speed of 55 miles per hour in an effort to force drivers to operate at a speed that maximized fuel efficiency. Gas was rationed at the

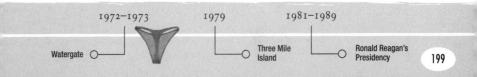

pump, and Americans' hands shook like those of your everyday meth addict while pumping the addictive fuel. Drivers whose license plate ended in an odd number were allowed to purchase gasoline on odd-numbered days. Drivers whose license plate ended in an even number were allowed to purchase gasoline on even numbered days. Despite the government's effort to control the flow of gasoline, long lines filled with angry and frustrated drivers became the norm.

On March 18, 1974, OPEC felt that its message had been heard and kindly lifted the embargo; oil from Arab countries began to flow back into the United States. Despite the lifting of the embargo, oil prices did not return to their pre-embargo levels, and it was not long before the memories of a full tank of gas and a Bee Gee's 8-track for under seven bucks was all but forgotten. This dance of hatred between oil-producing Arab nations and the United States continues on today with no realistic end in sight.

Understanding Israel

There are several lessons to be learned from the OPEC oil crisis but none more important than the need for Americans to understand the Arabs' Jewish neighbor. Unpopular with those it shares a border with, Israel has always enjoyed a near Canadian-like acceptance from the government of the United States. However, for Americans outside the confines of the federal government's inner circle, there is a lot about Israel that is misunderstood. For instance, why is Israel so hated by those around them, and really, what does kosher mean and how do you properly use the term in your day-to-day conversations?

Since hate is so hard to understand, it is best to just either go with it or ignore it, but kosher, that is something you can really wrap your head around. If you take the time to learn what is kosher, it's something you can impress your Jewish and non-Jewish friends with. To excel in using this term correctly,

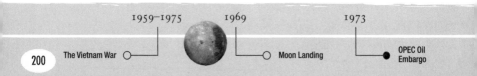

1959–1975   1969   1973

The Vietnam War   Moon Landing   OPEC Oil Embargo

you need to understand that the word *kosher* has made a successful transition into the world of American slang. It is important, therefore, that you learn to use the word properly outside of its original intended use. Like people, *kosher* has grown and matured, and to fully understand your Jewish neighbor you will need to grasp the full use of the word.

Please refrain from doing any further research with respect to the word *kosher*. It is important that this test be taken completely unaided by the benefits of studying. Upon completion of this short quiz you will not only have a better understanding about what is kosher but you will have a better understanding about how Jewish-friendly you really are.

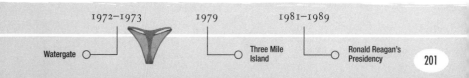

1972–1973   1979   1981–1989

Watergate   Three Mile Island   Ronald Reagan's Presidency

1. True or False: The use of a recognized rabbi to bless the food you are about to eat will in fact make the food kosher.

   a. True   b. False

2. Can Chinese food be considered kosher?

   a. Yes   b. No

3. If your best friend breaks up with his girlfriend, is it kosher for you to begin dating her after three months?

   a. Yes   b. No

4. If you are invited to two parties on the same night, is it kosher to lie to the host that you like the least and then attend the get-together at your preferred location?

   a. Yes   b. No

5. True or False: For meat to be considered kosher, the animal must be slaughtered in front of a certified rabbi.

   a. Yes   b. No

6. If you make a run to McDonald's to grab some lunch, and a couple of your friends ask you to pick something up for them, is it kosher for you to keep their change?

   a. Yes   b. No

1959–1975   1969   1973

The Vietnam War   Moon Landing   OPEC Oil Embargo

7. If you hook up one night with someone you met for the first time and the sex is lousy, is it kosher for you to ignore his or her phone calls?

        a. Yes   b. No

8. Which one of the following animals is not considered kosher?

        a. Cows   c. Bulls
        b. Sheep   d. Pigs

9. True or False: It is kosher to drink milk with your hamburger.

        a. Yes   b. No

10. It is kosher to sit along the front rail of a strip club and not tip?

        a. Yes   b. No

Answers

1. **B.** Although there are ritualistic prayers and blessings that a rabbi can give to bless the food, kosher is in the preparation, not the blessing. As a result, if the food is not kosher when it hits the table, it is too late. You will be eating kosher free that night.

2. **A.** Kosher food has nothing to do with the style of cooking from a particular country; it only has to do with how the food is prepared. There are all kinds of intelligent Chinese entrepreneurs across the country who understand that kosher fanatics will pay a premium for food that follows the tenets of the Torah. For most Chinese restaurants, it is the preparation of cat that they find most difficult to keep kosher.

3. **A.** Ninety days should be plenty of time for your buddy to get over her. If she was really that good between the sheets, he would have held on to her regardless of how little they have in common. If he needs more time, date around his back for the first thirty days to see if it works out. After that, he needs to just suck it up. After all, one man's trash is another man's treasure.

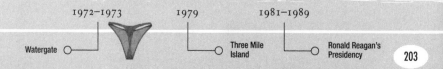

4. **B.** By lying to the host you like the least, you have disqualified any hope for kosher status. It would be kosher for you to attend the second party exclusively as long as you are up front with the other hostess and tell her you don't like her as much as the person hosting your preferred event.

5. **A.** Rabbis new to the profession or between synagogues often find themselves observing animal slaughters to earn a paycheck. No animal food can earn the distinction of kosher without the death of the animal being witnessed by a rabbi.

6. **A.** Fast-food runs are notorious for leaving the driver upside down in the transaction. There should be no debate. It is always kosher for the driver to keep the change.

7. **A.** Relationships can overcome a lot of things; however, bad sex is not one of them. Life is too short for you to spend with someone without any nighttime skills. Ignore the calls and move on.

8. **D.** The Torah states that for animal meat to be kosher, it has to not only have cloven hooves but also to chew the cud. The pig possesses split hooves, but unfortunately it doesn't chew the cud.

9. **B.** You can do a lot of things, but the Torah states, "You may not cook a young animal in the milk of its mother." You better grab a beer with that burger.

10. **B.** Absolutely not kosher. The ladies at these clubs work on tips and the premier seating along the rail of the stage is reserved for those who tip. The cover charge you paid at the door does get you in and entitles you to watch the show, but if you are not going to tip, you need to take a seat at one of the tables located several feet from the stage.

Please take a moment to add up your score and then take a look at the chart below to gauge your kosher intellect.

1–4 correct: By all accounts, you failed. Sorry, no retakes.

5–7 correct: Nice work. Go visit a Jewish delicatessen and have some lunch—you earned it.

8–10 correct: Congratulations! Find your lighter because you are lighting the Menorah next Hanukkah!

1959–1975   1969   1973

The Vietnam War   Moon Landing   OPEC Oil Embargo

WATERGATE

The Dick was crooked

Sounds Like a Scene from *Boogie Nights*

Anytime a historically significant event includes secret tapes, a hotel, someone named "Deep Throat," and a "Tricky Dick," it is sure to cause an explosive reaction. But despite the promising plot lines, this story is far removed from a discrete recording of a fetish-centered porn.

On June 17, 1972, five generally inept part-time burglars were arrested for their clumsy attempt to break into the Democratic National Committee Headquarters located in the Watergate hotel in Washington, D.C. This break-in wasn't your traditional smash-and-grab job that leaves behind the fingerprints of its perpetrators. Instead, it was an effort to see if the rumors about high-ranking Democratic Party officials wearing women's panties were in fact true, and to see if there was any other political dirt that could be used

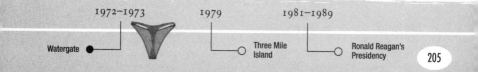

if President Richard Nixon's large lead in the polls did not hold up over the coming months.

In addition to the five amateurs who did the inside work, two more under-qualified criminals were arrested for being accomplices to the crime. All seven men were linked to an organization known as "CREEP," or committee to re-elect the president. Surely this committee and its plans were doomed to fail if their naming strategy session adjourned after agreeing on "CREEP."

Dick Obsessed

With the seven unusual suspects in orange jumpsuits indirectly linked to President Nixon, an investigation ensued. Among the reporters covering these events were Bob Woodward and Carl Bernstein of the *Washington Post*. During their investigation, they received a call from an anonymous informant code-named "Deep Throat," who pointed the journalists toward information linking President Nixon to the Watergate break-in. In 2005, Deep Throat was identi-fied as the not-so-sexy and more recently dead FBI deputy director, William Mark Felt Sr.

Secret Tapes Show Crooked Dick

As details of money laundering, slush funds, and political payoffs emerged the Senate promised to help the low-rated and rarely viewed C-Span television channel rebound from its dreadful Nielsen ratings report for the month of January. Keeping their promise as politicians rarely do, the Senate held hear-ings on the investigation from March 17 to August 7, 1973. The excitement was tremendous, as Americans were fixated with C-Span's HD coverage of the hearings. President Nixon was first dragged into the fray when Howard

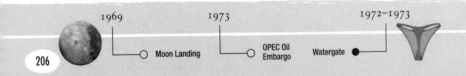

1969   1973   1972–1973

Moon Landing   OPEC Oil Embargo   Watergate

Baker of Tennessee famously asked, "What did the President know, and when did he know it?"

☞ *Shortly thereafter, Fred Thompson of **LAW AND ORDER** fame and failed 2008 Republican nominee, scored like a high school senior on prom night with the poignant question of whether or not there were listening devices in the White House, to which the answer was affirmative.* ☜ Upon hearing that there were, in fact, listening devices in the White House, Senate committee members nearly blew their load, and the tapes were quickly subpoenaed. Nixon immediately enacted Dick Cheney's "what happens in the White House stays in the White House" executive privilege. But investigators wanted the truth, even if they couldn't handle it. The issues of the tapes went all the way to the United States Supreme Court.

In a surprising and disappointing ruling for fans of partisan politics, the Supreme Court justices ruled unanimously that Nixon had to surrender the tapes. The released tapes covered Nixon and one of his aides planning a cover-up of the break-in, and having the CIA falsely claim that national security was at stake. Once the contents were revealed, ego boosting impeachment proceedings began. With the tapes released and the damage done, any allies Nixon had left had to admit the obvious: the Dick was crooked. President Nixon resigned ten days later.

Pardon Me?

Nixon's resignation catapulted Gerald Ford from the vice presidency to the commander in chief. As one of his first acts of duty for his country, President Gerald Ford granted Nixon a full and unconditional pardon for any crimes he may have committed while president. It was for all of his manipulation of the situation and attempts to escape blame, and not his ability to tie his unit in a knot, that earned Nixon the nearly enviable nickname of "Tricky Dick."

THREE MILE ISLAND

Off the consideration list for tourists

A Really, Really Exclusive Destination

Lacking the sandy beaches and sunshine that bring vacationers to popular island destinations, the city council for Three Mile Island spent years debating various ways to attract tourism to their Pennsylvania island. Local officials made an offer to Wayne Newton, but to no avail. ☞ *They were let down, too, when Blue Man Group and Céline Dion chose Vegas over their secret vacation hideaway.* ☜ Three Mile Island remained off the consideration list for street performers and island-loving tourists.

It was the spring of 1968, and as tourism continued to fail to meet expectations, the local government decided the time had come to focus on a nontraditional approach. They decided to focus on adventure tourism. They wanted to provide a vacation destination where people could generally feel safe but at the same time know they were only a few minutes from certain death if something

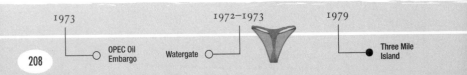

went unexpectedly wrong. It was decided that the easiest and most expensive way to accomplish this would be to build a full-time 24/7 nuclear reactor.

Tourist Trap

Three Mile Island quickly built a nuclear reactor on the banks of the Susquehanna River. This all-day every-day danger was popular among both full-time residents and island vacationers. ☞ *Local merchants sold scores of the popular souvenir, "I went to Three Mile Island and all I got was cancer and this lousy T-shirt."* ☜ The nuclear reactors on Three Mile Island accomplished exactly what they were intended to do. They filled the grid with much-needed electricity and the island's dilapidated Red Roof Inn with thrill-seeking tourists.

Many nonbelievers criticized the concept, stating the danger was a hoax. Fortunately, the danger proved real when one of the two nuclear reactors suffered a meltdown on March 28, 1979, releasing dangerous radioactive material into the island's atmosphere. The 25,000 people living within five miles of the reactor found themselves in imminent danger, and pregnant woman were told to flee as quickly as possible to avoid birthing babies the size of sea cows.

Death Count

With the aggressive reporting of the alphabet networks and Geraldo Rivera filing reports from inside the breached reactor, Americans were anxious to find out what the final death count was for America's first nuclear accident.

After careful consideration, it was determined that no lives were lost in this accident. And although one of the two reactors was permanently shut down, adventure-loving vacationers were still able to make the trip to Three Mile Island, now exposing themselves to less than almost certain death.

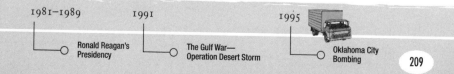

1981–1989 Ronald Reagan's Presidency

1991 The Gulf War— Operation Desert Storm

1995 Oklahoma City Bombing

RONALD REAGAN'S PRESIDENCY

Hollywood's own favorite Republican

Reading for a Role as President

With President Jimmy Carter giving the country economy-busting double-digit interest rates, cripplingly high inflation, and a slate of failed policies, America was thirsty for change during the former peanut farmer's re-election campaign of 1980. Challenging Carter and his lack of success was Hollywood's own favorite Republican, Ronald Reagan.

Reagan gathered his domestic and foreign policy experience on the sets of movies like *This Is the Army* and *Bedtime for Bonzo*, and to a lesser extent, as a two-term governor in the state of California. Even without Austrian-born bodybuilder Arnold Schwarzenegger's trademark grunts (now a big part of today's California governor's office), Reagan was widely viewed as the great communicator. Playing to win and not just to place, Reagan selected Texas

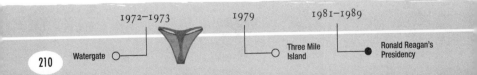

1972–1973
Watergate

1979
Three Mile Island

1981–1989
Ronald Reagan's Presidency

businessman and Republican Party Primary loser George H. W. Bush to be his running mate. Because of the U.S. state of affairs at the time, plus a home-field advantage in two of the largest states, the Reagan-Bush ticket easily took the election.

Jodie Foster Drove Me Crazy

Reagan took office in January 1981, with his wife, Nancy, and her "just say no to drugs" mantra by his side. Sixty-nine days after taking office and becoming the desire of aging widows across the country, Reagan was shot outside the Washington Hilton following a speaking engagement. ☞ *Immediate speculation was that it might be the bitter and jealous actor Michael Landon from* **Little House on the Prairie** *who had pulled the trigger.* ☜ However, within seconds of the shots being fired, the pride of Texas, John Warnock Hinckley Jr., was found holding the .22 caliber gun used in the assassination attempt. Hinckley's reason for the assault: he wanted to gain the attention of Jodie Foster, whom he saw in the movie *Taxi Driver*. Unfortunately for Hinckley, Foster didn't like men the way Sharon Stone likes men; she liked men the way a sister is supposed to like her brother. Foster's personal top ten list of most desirable was full of people who peed sitting down.

Even with a bullet from a mentally ill drifter in his lung, Reagan managed to keep the sense of humor that had endeared him to the American public intact. Reportedly while on a gurney, with the bullet still inside him, he asked the young nurse who held his hand "Does Nancy know about us?" And as he went into surgery to have the bullet removed, he gamely told the surgeon, "I hope you are a Republican."

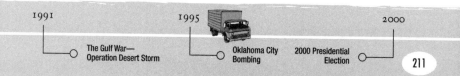

1991   1995   2000

The Gulf War—
Operation Desert Storm

Oklahoma City
Bombing

2000 Presidential
Election

Two Terms for the Gipper

Following his recovery from his assassination attempt, Reagan completed his two-term presidency, opposing Communism at every turn and often referring to the Soviet Union as the Evil Empire. He endeared himself to the very wealthy by cutting their taxes in support of his trickle-down economic plan. He rebuilt our military while advocating for peace through strength. Sadly, President Reagan lost his fight against Alzheimer's on June 5, 2004.

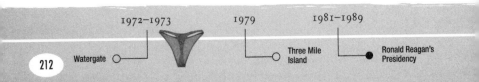

1972–1973

Watergate

1979

Three Mile
Island

1981–1989

Ronald Reagan's
Presidency

1991

THE GULF WAR—
OPERATION DESERT STORM

The presidential handbook on dealing with tyrannical leaders

Saddam Goes on the Offensive

Using an outdated Islamic decision matrix that showed leaders of the not-so-free Arab world when it was acceptable to trade oil for virgins, Iraqi president and deflowerer Saddam Hussein ordered his military to overrun the oil-rich but nearly defenseless nation of Kuwait. Since Kuwait was part of the Ottoman Empire up until 1899, which at the time was controlled by Iraq, it was obvious that ninety years later Hussein was justified in his reacquisition of the neighboring country. Best of all was that because Hussein could demonstrate that Kuwait had Iraqi heritage, all of the oil pumped out of Kuwait was subject to virgin trading.

Hussein was looking for something fresh, hoping to use a portion of his new trading commodity to score a fistful of virgins of the Western variety. For weeks he had been enjoying sleepless nights, with thoughts of a blonde

1991

The Gulf War—
Operation Desert Storm

1995

Oklahoma City
Bombing

2000 Presidential
Election

2000

213

American-made bombshell from Arizona being first up, even if he had to overpay.

Despite Hussein's obvious right to take over Kuwait for his own sexual self-interest, the world community was irate. Pleading on behalf of virgins worldwide, the famous and former American virgin Britney Spears, who later explained that "Justin may have touched me but he was never in me," begged for a coordinated global response to remove Saddam from Kuwait, thus protecting the virginity of scores of young women worldwide. ☞ *Under pressure from record executives who feared that too much public speaking would expose Britney's subpar IQ, the United Nations, at the urging of the United States, began to discuss the need to liberate the country of Kuwait.* ✐

Good in This Life and the Next

After calculating that with Kuwait's oil combined with Iraq's oil he could trade for more virgins than his appetite could satisfy, Hussein set up a secondary market for virgin trading as he approached the leaders of martyr-rich countries. As part of the religious tradition, Islamic suicide bombers are guaranteed a healthy helping of seventy-two virgins when they enter heaven for their deadly act.

Seeing a supply and demand match, Hussein ordered that the oil being pumped from Kuwaiti oil fields be increased dramatically and immediately. This closely controlled secondary market, along with the fear that Hussein might order his military to parade right through Kuwait and on into Saudi Arabia, giving him control of approximately 40 percent of the world's known oil reserves, inspired global action.

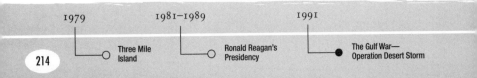

1979 — Three Mile Island

1981–1989 — Ronald Reagan's Presidency

1991 — The Gulf War— Operation Desert Storm

You Need a Signed Permission Slip

Hearing from others that this scenario could be devastating to the American economy, Bush consulted the presidential handbook on dealing with tyrannical leaders in oil-rich countries. Acting on the advice from this little-known handbook, Bush decided to go on the attack. Unfortunately for Bush, in a world of instant gratification, he could not attack Iraq without approval from either the United Nations or the United States Congress. Anxious, Bush impatiently launched Operation Desert Shield, selling it as a mission to protect freedom and liberty as instructed by the handbook. The reality was he wanted troops in place to act swiftly and aggressively once he inevitably received permission from the United Nations to go on the offensive.

During the process of obtaining U.N. approval, the United States put together an impressive coalition that included thirty-nine other countries, most of which ignored martyrdom for sexual gain. Coalition forces gave Hussein a January 15, 1991, deadline to remove all of his encroaching forces from sovereign Kuwaiti soil, which in turn would settle down the oil-for-virgin marketplace. As January 15 came and went with no Iraqi cooperation, the conflict began two days later on January 17, 1991.

Allied forces included but were not limited to Australia, Afghanistan, Argentina, Canada, Czechoslovakia, Denmark, Egypt, Germany, Greece, Hungary, Saudi Arabia, South Korea, Spain, Syria, and the United Kingdom. Rumor has it Niger and Oman were listed on the roster of allied forces, too; however, it is now believed that it may have been a clerical error as White House officials continue to try and prove their existence.

At 3:00 A.M., under the cover of darkness, coalition forces began an all-out air assault on Iraqi forces and their military instillations. U.S. jets and more U.S. jets and more U.S. jets, along with the occasional British jet, relentlessly pounded strategic Iraqi targets. Huddled around satellite imagery, commander

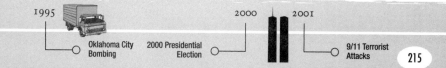

1995   Oklahoma City   2000 Presidential   2000   2001   9/11 Terrorist
        Bombing   Election   Attacks

of the allied forces General Norman Schwarzkopf enjoyed the bright lights and fires that were beamed back to command center. Not easily bored, Schwarzkopf ordered thirty-eight consecutive days of the nearly nonstop air assault. Unable to defend itself from the aerial festivities, the Iraqi military attempted to widen the war by launching unreliable Soviet-engineered Scud missiles into Saudi Arabia and the unpopular nation of Israel.

Hussein believed most Arab nations had been looking for another reason to re-engage military hostilities with the all-but-ostracized Israelis, and if they fired back, Hussein's Muslim brothers would be forced to have his back and abandoned their support of the coalition. Much to the surprise of everyone, the Israelis grinned and bore it, refraining from retaliating and thus keeping the coalition intact and the pressure on Iraq.

You Don't Have to Go Home, But Get the Hell Out of Here

On February 24, 1991, Schwarzkopf's boredom meter sounded, and he sent ground troops into Iraq. Demoralized by the constant bombings from the air over the last two and a half months, tens of thousands of Iraqi soldiers eagerly surrendered. ☞ *As the white flags came out, Hussein ordered his troops to pack up their shit and get the hell out of Kuwait.* ☜ With the remaining Iraqi soldiers happy to be alive and leaving Kuwait, one at a time in single file, coalition forces ended efforts exactly 100 hours after the ground attack began.

As Kuwait was returned to the Kuwaitis and Hussein's attempt to enlarge the oil-for-virgins marketplace beyond its capacity was thwarted, Britney Spears announced that out of fear for Hussein's plan, she had gone ahead and gave Justin her virginity, effectively taking her off of Hussein's radar. ☞ *By all accounts, the night was magical, inspiring her to sing someone else's lyrics to her hit song "Hit Me Baby One More Time."* ☜

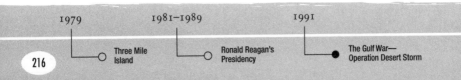

1979 — Three Mile Island

1981–1989 — Ronald Reagan's Presidency

1991 — The Gulf War— Operation Desert Storm

1995

OKLAHOMA CITY BOMBING

Hiding behind their radical beliefs

Timmy & Terry: Army Surplus Terrorists

Born without fanfare on April 23, 1968, Timothy McVeigh entered the world like all white males do, with considerable advantages over women and minorities. He parlayed these advantages into a relatively distinguished yet short military career in the U.S. Army from 1988 until 1991. Highlighting his service was his tour of duty during the Gulf War. During his days of basic training, Timothy met up with another white male who was born under the paparazzi radar, Terry Nichols. Nichols was an unsuccessful husband whose second marriage was to a mail-order bride seeking a green card. Despite Nichols' issues within his own household, he proved, unfortunately, to be a capable wingman in domestic terrorism.

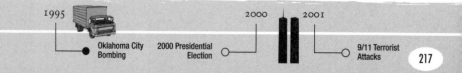

1995 — Oklahoma City Bombing
2000 — 2000 Presidential Election
2001 — 9/11 Terrorist Attacks

Did You Say Waco or Wacko?

The domestic terrorism tandem of Tim and Terry claimed that the government's handling of the Branch Davidian situation at Waco warranted a response. Hiding behind their radical beliefs in their version of God and the Second Amendment, the BDs stockpiled a large amount of weapons at their religious compound. After being tipped off by a UPS driver turned honorable and responsible crime stopper, Alcohol, Tobacco and Firearms agents paid a visit to the organization's facility near Waco, Texas. With the welcome mat rolled up, a fifty-one day standoff ensued. The conflict ended when seventy-six followers of the Branch Davidians died inside the compound from a self-inflicted fire set by the weapon stockpilers themselves. For Tim and Terry, the government was to blame.

Execution

After months of planning and bomb building, Timothy rented a Ryder Truck in Junction City, Kansas, under the fictitious name of Robert D. Kling, smartly opting for the damage-waiver option on the vehicle. Over the next few days, McVeigh and Nichols loaded the truck up with 7,000 pounds of deadly explosives. As a frame of reference for what 7,000 pounds of explosives looks like, it is the equivalent of thirty-five Oprah Winfrey's, circa 2008.

On April 19, 1995, with Timothy in the driver's seat and Nichols electing not to ride shotgun, the American-born terrorist parked the explosive-filled truck in the underground parking lot of the Alfred P. Murrah Federal Building in Oklahoma City, Oklahoma. At 9:02 A.M., as Timothy calmly made his way to the getaway car parked a few blocks away, the rental truck exploded. The blast was so significant that the front of the building was completely blown away and the explosion itself was felt over fifty-five miles away. The damage

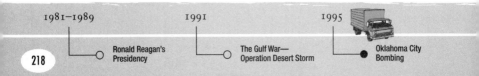

1981–1989   Ronald Reagan's Presidency

1991   The Gulf War— Operation Desert Storm

1995   Oklahoma City Bombing

was catastrophic and at the end of the day, 168 people were dead and more than 800 were injured.

Less than two hours after the deadly attack, Timothy was picked up by an Oklahoma state trooper. ☞ *His alleged offense was driving the get-away car without a tag and for having a concealed weapon on him, Plaxico Burress-style.* ✍ As the FBI was piecing together McVeigh's guilt, a couple of days later Nichols turned himself in and agreed to turn on Timothy as quickly as he was asked.

With a mountain of evidence against him and his wingman chirping, Timothy was sentenced to death by lethal injection. The deadly needle was inserted on April 19, 1995. For his trouble, Nichols received 168 consecutive life sentences, making him eligible for parole sometime long after his death.

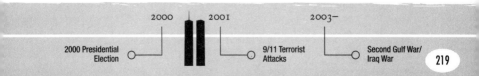

2000

2001

2003—

2000 Presidential Election

9/11 Terrorist Attacks

Second Gulf War/ Iraq War

219

2000 PRESIDENTIAL ELECTION

George W. was their guy, even if he was one whiskey sour from falling off the wagon

The Prize

Sure, being president of the United States is a cool job. But coming off the shenanigans of a Clinton administration, it rivaled the casting director's job at Vivid Videos. Impeachment aside, the Clinton years showed us that even when your wife is pissed about you dropping bombs on small but overpopulated African countries, you can still find young, overweight interns willing to offer up late-night oral.

For George W. Bush and Al Gore, the opportunity to intimidate nearly defenseless foreign countries that had yet to embrace democracy was overwhelming. They garnered the support of their wealthy friends and made promises they never intended to keep for the opportunity to see how far their sexual mojo would take them with their own staff of willing young interns.

1991   1995   2000

The Gulf War—
Operation Desert Storm

Oklahoma City
Bombing

2000 Presidential
Election

The Controversy

Everything leading up to Election Day, November 7, 2000, pointed to an extremely close result and record voter turnout. Not because Americans were excited about the candidates, but because for the first time in election history voters received goody bags filled with candy, condoms, and scratch-off tickets. As polls closed on the East Coast, and results began to filter in, it became apparent that Florida's twenty-five Electoral College votes would determine the election. ☞ *At stake was the right to invite friends and campaign contributors to sleep in the Lincoln bedroom, as well as the power to give out meaningless, well-paying government jobs to unqualified college friends over the next four years.* ☜

At 7:48 P.M., NBC declared friend of Mother Earth, Al Gore, the winner in Florida. Two minutes later, CBS and CNN followed suit, and by 8:02, all five major networks declared Gore the winner. But like Paris Hilton's publicist, Gore couldn't catch a break.

He had to deal with the fact that the governor of Florida was Bush's younger brother, and Florida's secretary of state, Katherine Harris (who appeared to have an epic crush on the Bush brothers), was responsible for certifying Florida's election results. Hours later, in an ironic twist, big brother George W. was announced the winner of Florida and bottles of nonalcoholic champagne began popping as the Texas governor and recovering alcoholic was announced the president-elect.

☞ *Unfortunately for Bush, his announced margin of victory was Kate Moss thin, and an automatic recount was ordered.* ☜ As a result, a time-out was called and the verdict as to the winner of the 2000 presidential election was delayed for thirty days.

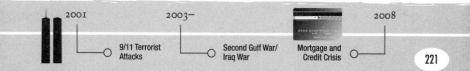

2001

2003—

2008

9/11 Terrorist Attacks

Second Gulf War/ Iraq War

Mortgage and Credit Crisis

221

Thirty Days of Nonsense

Even though Gore had clearly won the national popular vote, it is the Electoral College that actually determines the presidency. Unlike regular college, where truckloads of alcohol contribute to questionable decision making, including, but not limited to, participation in post-party threesomes, the Electoral College is not really a college at all. No campus, no classes, no degrees to be earned. Instead, it is an organization responsible for making sure the poor and poorly informed do not get in the way of the perceived right of those with more money to elect the president.

The Electoral College vote was so close that the Democratic Party requested that Katherine Harris delay certifying the election results until a manual hand recount could be completed.

Unfortunately for the Democrats, Harris was one of eight cochairs for the Republican Party's Florida election, and granting the request would make it nearly impossible for her to marry into the Bush family at a later date. She quickly dismissed their request and planned to certify Bush the winner and hand him the magical twenty-five remaining electoral votes. With no cooperation from Harris, Democrats quickly looked to the Florida Supreme Court for relief. And relief is what they got.

The Florida Supreme Court ruled that watching election officials debate the differences between hanging chads and pregnant chads in determining voter intent made for hilarious television viewing and that the election should not be certified until manual recounts were completed. However, realizing this decision would likely reverse Bush's lead and crown Gore the winner, Republicans filed suit with the United States Supreme Court, arguing that network television already provided hilarious programming, and that the comedy surrounding the manual recount was redundant and should be stopped.

1991

1995

2000

The Gulf War—
Operation Desert Storm

Oklahoma City
Bombing

2000 Presidential
Election

King George, Says the Supreme Court

After more than 100 million Americans inconvenienced themselves to vote, the only votes that counted were those of the six white guys, two white woman, and the black man sitting on the United States Supreme Court. Not exactly a cross section of our diverse nation.

Resting comfortably on their lifetime appointments, the nine Supreme Court justices brought partisan politics to the forefront and voted 5–4 down party lines to stop the manual recount in Florida. Once again, bottles of non-alcoholic champagne began popping as the Supreme Court effectively handed George W. the presidency.

The Election Party Is Over

To Republicans, it did not matter that every vote in Florida was not counted. It only mattered that more Republican votes were counted. They did not care if Daddy Bush pulled some strings or whether Brother Bush promised Harris any late-night favors. George W. was their guy, even if he was one whiskey sour from falling off the wagon.

Democrats, on the other hand, were left with mixed emotions. Although furious over the manner in which they lost the White House, they were ecstatic about the job they did in winning the popular vote with one of the least likeable candidates in history. They ran a cardboard cutout against the son of a former president and actually got more votes.

As for the rest of us, we just rolled with it. George W. gave us lower taxes and higher carbon monoxide levels. Al probably would have given us higher taxes and more green space. At the end of the day, we moved on. ☞ *For most Americans, it doesn't really matter who is tapping the ass of the interns in the oval office, just as long as someone is.* ☜

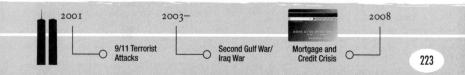

George W. Bush
1600 Pennsylvania Ave.
Washington, DC 20500
1 (202) whi-skey
offthebottle@dadscoattails.com

Objective

Seeking a position that allows me to run up enormous amounts of debt, take frequent vacations, and have no accountability for any of my decisions.

Employment History

President, United States of America, 2001–2009

Talking marionette for Dick Cheney. Came to the aid of Cheney when it was determined he was too crusty and not likeable enough to be elected president himself. Not required to have a thought of my own as Dick made all the decisions.

On behalf of Dick, helped the richest 2 percent of Americans.

On behalf of Dick, created cool deck of cards full of Iraqi enemies.

Took longest presidential "vacation" *ever* when Dick laid me off.

First recovering alcoholic to be elected president. (I was a drunk long before I knew Dick.)

Governor, Texas, 1994–2000

With the help of an army of influential people, was handed the keys to the Texas governor's office.

Brought about legislative change allowing oil companies to pollute the environment more freely.

Borrowed billions of dollars so that the debt could be passed down to generations of Texans.

The great executioner. Set all time record for executions for a single governor.

Part Owner and Managing Partner,
Texas Rangers Major League Baseball, 1989–1994
Traded Sammy Sosa for some crap after realizing there was no room in the middle of the Ranger lineup for a guy to hit 600-plus homeruns.

Appeared on Jumbotron 1989.

Did what I was told 1990.

Left important decisions to others.

Chief Executive Officer,
Business disaster after business disaster, 1979–1989
Let's just say I headed up a couple of companies that were not as successful as I would have liked. I ran up billions, yes with a *B*, in debt and was bailed out by family and friends.

Town Drunk, 1967–1972
I used to party harder than the Kennedys.

Reference:

Kenneth Lay, Former Enron Executive

Albert Arnold Gore Jr.
4743 Environmental Lane
Mother Earth, Mother Earth 32946
(463) Go-Green
iheartcockroaches@motherearth.com

Objectives

As a political cyborg with a passion for the environment, I plan on stopping deforestation and providing clean air and water to all of earth's inhabitants, including the cute and lovable chipmunks. With a human form and a computerized brain, my success is inevitable.

Employment History

President, Victims of a Partisan U.S. Supreme Court While Seeking Public Office, 2001–Present

Following loss to George W. Bush in the 2000 election, I started this not-for-profit company in an attempt to combat the political influence of the right wing in the United States Supreme Court and provide support for any and all left-wing extremists who encounter unfavorable decisions from the high court while seeking public office in the future.

After five years and no clients I feel I have a lot of time on my hands.

Grew a beard to increase "hippie cred."

As president of the company, I require staff to call me Mr. President, and it feels real good.

Vice President, United States, 1993–2001

I was the man behind the man for eight years. I proved to the country that I can keep a secret. Enjoyed Clinton's impeachment hearing, and was indifferent with the result.

Played "Yang" to Clinton's "Yin."

Invented the Internet (damn, I'm good).

Hung the moon and the sun.

Senator, United States, 1984–1993

Uneventful and boring, just the way I like it. Continued to cheat on Tipper with Mother Earth. Goodness I love her, so green, leafy, and full of water with a salty aftertaste.

Proposed legislation requiring Ted Kennedy to recycle his beer cans. (1985)

Proposed legislation requiring Ted Kennedy to recycle his liquor bottles. (1989)

Proposed legislation requiring Ted Kennedy to recycle bottles and cans from his mixers. (1992)

Congressman, United States House of Representatives, 1976–1982

Feel free to omit above position when considering my resume, as I accomplished very little in those six years.

Reference:

Mother Earth. Of course.

2001

9/11 TERRORIST ATTACKS

Public enemy number one

An Evil Plot

Armed with box cutters and a deep-rooted hatred for America, fifteen men from Saudi Arabia, two from the United Arab Emirates, one from Egypt, and one from Lebanon bordered four civil airliners on the morning of September 11, 2001, with the intention of meeting Mohammad and the seventy-two virgins promised to each of them for their cowardly homicidal actions that were to follow.

The nineteen terrorists were the chosen foot soldiers, following years of planning to strike at the heart of the American community. The masterminds of the attacks were safely tucked away in less-than-luxurious caves in the mountain region of Afghanistan, watching the horrific events unfold on satellite television. Unable to acquire the weapons necessary to cause enormous destruction in the United States, the Al Qaida think tank opted for commer-

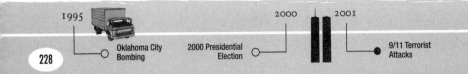

1995
Oklahoma City
Bombing

2000 Presidential
Election

2000

2001

9/11 Terrorist
Attacks

cial aircrafts full of aviation fuel to act as the missiles they desperately desired. With their irrational dislike for the United States as their motivation, the Islamist terrorists hijacked four cross-country flights, taking over their cockpits and turning the aircrafts into weapons of war.

American Airlines Flight 11

American Airlines flight 11 left Boston, Massachusetts, en route to Los Angeles, California, carrying eighty-one passengers and eleven crew members. Fifteen minutes into the flight, five of those passengers ignored the "stay seated with your seat belt securely fastened signs" and instead went from fare paying passengers to hijackers as they took over the plane.

Mohamed Atta, one of the hijackers, put the flight-training skills he had recently acquired from a Venice, Florida, aviation school to work as he turned the plane away from its scheduled flight plan and instead headed toward New York City, the financial capital of the United States. Traveling at approximately 466 miles per hour, at 8:46 A.M., Atta navigated the plane into his desired destination, the north tower of the World Trade Center. Flight 11 made impact between floors ninety-three and ninety-nine, killing all on board instantly. Immediately, media speculation was that pilot error must be to blame for the tragedy.

United Flight 175

That same morning, United flight 175 left Logan International airport with a planned arrival for LAX in Los Angeles, California. Carrying fifty-six passengers and nine crew members, the plane was fortunately far from being filled to capacity. Playing the role of Mohamed Atta on this flight was United Arab Emirates non-Christian Marwan al-Shehhi, one of Atta's flight school

2003—

Second Gulf War/
Iraq War

2008

Mortgage and
Credit Crisis

The 2008
Election

229

companions and a member of his T-Mobile "myFaves." At 8:52 A.M., a "the sky's the limit when you put your mind to it" male flight attendant contacted United Airlines' San Francisco office to report the hijacking.

Eleven minutes later, at approximately 9:03 A.M., flight 175, traveling at a speed of 545 miles per hour, struck the neighboring south tower of the World Trade Center, instantly killing all on board along with hundreds of "must get to work on time" Trade Center employees. Immediately, speculation of pilot error for flight 11 ceased as the media began to report that the United States was under attack.

American Flight 77

American Airlines flight 77 left Washington Dulles airport on a direct, non-stop flight to sunny Los Angeles, California, with five American-hating terrorists on board. Thirty minutes into the flight, with a belief that they were doing Allah's work, the five terrorists took control of the aircraft.

Receiving his flight training in the comfort of the Middle East–like heat of Scottsdale, Arizona, Atta and al-Shehhi's counterpart Hani Hanjour took over the piloting of the plane. Ignoring the star power of Los Angeles and its famous residents, Hanjour abandoned the Washington to Los Angeles American Airlines itinerary in favor of his own Washington to Pentagon itinerary. Before he had a chance to change his mind about taking a Hollywood stars bus tour, at approximately 9:37 A.M., he slammed the plane into the western portion of the Pentagon at a speed of 540 miles per hour, killing all sixty-four passengers, crew, and terrorists along with another 125 employees and visitors inside the Pentagon.

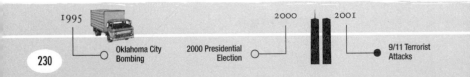

1995

Oklahoma City
Bombing

2000 Presidential
Election

2000

2001

9/11 Terrorist
Attacks

United Flight 93

United Airlines flight 93 left Newark, New Jersey, on a scheduled flight to the rainbow-flag-appreciating city of San Francisco, California. Onboard were thirty-seven passengers and seven crew members. Approximately forty minutes into the flight, the terrorists mobilized and secured control of the plane.

Once in control, Lebanese-born Ziad Jarrah entered the cockpit, taking on the duties of pilot despite not being on the United Airlines payroll. The hijackers herded the passengers to the back of the plane, where several of them began to make calls to family and friends to inform them of their situation. During these conversations, the passengers of flight 93 learned the sobering news that other planes had been hijacked earlier in the morning and used as missiles.

Realizing that the terrorists were on a suicide mission, the passengers revolted and attempted to take back control of the plane. As the confrontation became more intense, the hijackers abandoned their plans to crash the plane into the speculated target of either the White House or United States Capitol building and instead brought the plane down in a rural area of Stonycreek Township in Somerset County, Pennsylvania. With the impact measured at 563 miles per hour, all on board died instantly.

Meet Osama Bin Laden

With the country under attack with passenger airliners as the weapon of choice, all flights throughout the United States were grounded and those currently in the air were ordered to land immediately at the nearest airport so government officials could get a handle on the developing situation. Speculation of who was behind these acts of terrorism immediately turned to Osama Bin Laden. The Saudi Arabian national quickly became public enemy number one.

2003—

Second Gulf War/
Iraq War

Mortgage and
Credit Crisis

2008

The 2008
Election

As rescue efforts continued in Manhattan at the World Trade Center, both the North and South towers crumbled to the ground under the intense heat from the raging fires. With four passenger planes crashed, two towers down, and the Pentagon severely damaged, the death toll rose to a chilling 2,976 people. With the world on our side, the American people demanded that President George W. Bush prepare an immediate and unmeasured response to the most devastating acts of terrorism ever experienced on American soil.

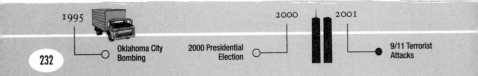

1995

2000

2001

Oklahoma City
Bombing

2000 Presidential
Election

9/11 Terrorist
Attacks

SECOND GULF WAR/ IRAQ WAR

A desert vacation gone wrong

Viva Iraq

When it comes time to get away from it all and really let loose, Las Vegas has been the preferred vacation destination for adult men for years. The bright lights, the gambling, the alcohol, and the disproportionate number of insanely hot girls has pulled men into this desert oasis for decades.

Despite the fact that Vegas offers every vice anyone could ever want, in 2003, the Middle East–obsessed triad of Republican leadership, Bush, Cheney, and Rumsfeld, began making plans for hundreds of thousands of their closest military friends to visit their preferred sand pit in the sun, Iraq. The thoughts of women all veiled up and covered from head to toe along with the lure of oil-driven riches proved to be irresistible for the three fun-loving pals with an infection of neocondral disease.

2003–

Second Gulf War/
Iraq War

2008

Mortgage and
Credit Crisis

The 2008
Election

233

Prelude to a Military Kiss

Much like a gambler with a propensity for addiction, the Bush family had been to Iraq once before and couldn't wait to get back. The First Gulf War ended in 1991 when former president George Bush Sr. negotiated the end of the conflict with a cease-fire. Bush the elder got most of what he wanted from his excursion to the desert, but like that one casino where you suffered from Reginald Denny–like luck, Bush didn't have a perfect trip either. In this case, Saddam Hussein was left in power because when Iraqi troops fled Kuwait, Bush had no mandate from the United Nations to order the United States military to march into Baghdad and forcibly remove the America-hating dictator. Disappointed but not completely deterred, Bush ordered coalition forces to pack up and come home.

☞ *During the Clinton presidency, Bush, the story-telling senior, would relay accounts of his fantastic trip to the Iraqi desert oasis.*

☜ Between AA meetings, George Jr. heard fantastic tales of easy wars and surging political popularity and thought if he was ever in a position to go, he would do just that.

Getting to the Desert, Whatever It Takes

When the U.S. Supreme Court handed the presidency to George Bush Jr. in the 2000 election, they effectively put George in the position to fulfill his dreams of the kind of desert invasion, his father had enjoyed. Plus, he wanted to get back at that casino that was so unlucky for his father and remove Saddam Hussein from power. With his commitment unwavering, George began poking around, looking for an excuse to order an Iraqi vacation.

In the aftermath of the September 11, 2001, attacks Bush and his desert-hungry companions, Cheney and Rumsfeld, saw an opportunity. No attention

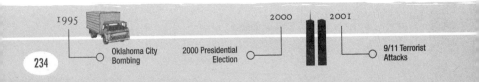

1995   2000   2001

Oklahoma City Bombing   2000 Presidential Election   9/11 Terrorist Attacks

was paid to the fact that it wasn't a great reason, as there was no direct link between Hussein and the 9/11 attacks. Nonetheless, it was still a reason. In response to the attacks, on September 20, 2001, George announced his new "War on Terror" along with the "Bush Jr. Doctrine," a philosophy of pre-emptive military action. ☞ *Much like a husband remarking to his wife that the guys are going to Vegas in June, Bush was setting the table for his trip.* ☜

The United States Makes Up a Story

Looking for foreign travel companions, Bush approached the United Nations about joining him on his proposed trip to Iraq. He tried to entice them with thoughts of hot, skin-blistering temperatures, but nearly everyone turned him down. Not deterred, Bush, along with his puppet, Prime Minister Tony Blair of Great Britain, ignored the need for a U.N. blessing for their travel plans and instead pumped America up for war. Looking out for his friends and former colleagues at Halliburton, Dick Cheney beat the drum of war nonstop until the United States Congress passed a resolution in October 2002, authorizing the use of force against Iraq.

To justify the offensive to the American people, George stated that the invasion was necessary to disarm Iraq of its weapons of mass destruction, end Saddam's support of terrorism, and free the people of Iraq, hoping Americans would buy at least two out of the three. Frustrated by the lack of international support for bringing hell to Baghdad, Bush and Blair were left with only a small coalition of the willing that included the ass-kissing nations of Spain, Italy, Poland, Australia, and Denmark when hostilities commenced in March 2003.

2003–
Second Gulf War/
Iraq War

2008
Mortgage and
Credit Crisis

The 2008
Election

The Morning After

The aftermath is the stuff of recent legend. Bush famously stood in front of an enormous "Mission Accomplished" banner while on the deck of the aircraft carrier USS *Lincoln* for a televised speech on May 1, 2003. Oddly enough, despite George announcing the end of major combat operations in the war with Iraq, as of 2009, U.S. troops were still deployed in Iraq, heroically continuing to try to accomplish the mission he said was accomplished.

To date, no weapons of mass destruction have been located in Iraq and the smoking gun between Hussein and 9/11 has never been established. American taxpayers continue to spend billions of dollars a month on the war, as the country's credibility in the international community is at an all-time low.

☞ *Unlike a Vegas vacationer whose alcohol-fueled exploits result in waking up broke, full of regret, and in the same bed as a dead hooker, Bush Jr., Cheney, and Rumsfeld make no apology for their desert vacation gone wrong.* ☜

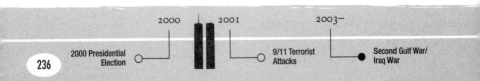

2000 — 2000 Presidential Election

2001 — 9/11 Terrorist Attacks

2003 — Second Gulf War/ Iraq War

2008

MORTGAGE AND CREDIT CRISIS

Credit standards as loose as Tara Reid

WTF?

What the fuck just happened? These were the five words echoing across every city and town, big or small, throughout the United States during 2008. No state was insulated from this un-God-like question. One minute Americans were pulling the equity out of their rapidly inflating homes to purchase a gas-guzzling Hummer, and the next minute they were accessing the line of credit tied to their home to go to Vegas and buy a Vegas-style hummer from a working girl wearing a short skirt and carrying a small purse.

At the time, nothing seemed wrong with the spending. Every month, home values were appreciating significantly with no real end in sight. That was until chairman of the Federal Reserve Ben Bernanke's head reappeared from his ass. As the country's financial system was blowing up in front of us and Middle America was demanding answers, some politicians and Wall Street executives

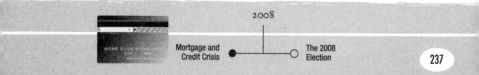

2008

Mortgage and
Credit Crisis

The 2008
Election

237

were trying to deflect the possibility of investigations into the meltdown. As is the case more often than not, the whole thing started with someone's short-sighted good intentions.

Houses for Everyone!

One of the goals of both the Clinton and Bush administration was to increase home ownership among Americans. Henry Cisneros, Clinton's top housing advisor, in accordance with Clinton's goals of increased home ownership, loosened the mortgage restrictions for first-time home buyers, enabling them to buy a house they could never afford. In conjunction with the loosening standards, low interest rates coupled with huge sums of cash from foreign investors made credit easier than the captain of the cheerleading team to obtain. "Zero percent financing" and "no interest, no payments for five years" became standard procedure for consumers who might or might not be qualified for such regal treatment.

Although Clinton and Cisneros got the ball started, the Bush administration kept the good times rolling for homeowners and consumers. The home ownership rate, which had hovered around 64 percent for Americans from 1980 until 1994, began to rise. In 2004, this number peaked at almost 70 percent. Many of these loans were being made to people who would not be able to pay the loan back, earning the dubious "subprime loan" label.

☞ *IN 2007, before the "who can shit the bed bigger and better" dueling stock market and housing market crashes, it seemed every American had one or more houses.* ☜ Even people without jobs had vacation homes, investment properties, and old-fashioned mistress-meeting condos. Cisneros, one of the architects of the mess, got caught mistress-meeting in his and was forced to leave office in 1997. As for Clinton, he was more of a home-office adulterer, using the oval office as his on-the-side location.

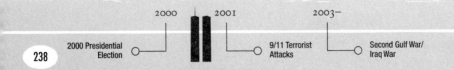

2000   2001   2003–

2000 Presidential Election   9/11 Terrorist Attacks   Second Gulf War/ Iraq War

Bubblelicious

As home ownership and demand rose as fast as a gaydar around Ryan Seacrest, so did housing prices. With increased demand for housing, and credit standards as loose as Tara Reid, home prices began to skyrocket in 2006. Americans began to think real estate prices could only go up as fast as Jenna Haze could go down, and they acted accordingly. As home prices increased, Americans used their homes like piggy banks, taking the equity out of their house again and again to fuel outrageous spending habits. Immediate gratification was the order of the day, as well as a neighborly game of "Can you top this?"

Regulatory changes allowed mortgage originators to sell their loans to other institutions. These mortgages were often sold off in groups, disguising the real risk behind some of the riskier borrowers. Credit rating agencies like Standard and Poors rated these packaged loan products AAA—their highest safety rating. With the ability to quickly pass packaged loans off to somebody else, loan underwriting standards became nearly unnecessary. Nobody seemed to care if the home buyer was unqualified, as long as it blew up on somebody else.

Underwriters were pressured to inflate home values to help push loans through. Home buyers with no job, no income, and no assets became known as "Ninja Loans" in the industry. "No doc" loans and "Stated Income" loans allowed borrowers to make up any number for their annual income in order to fit the house they wanted. To make things even more comical, two-thirds of these subprime loans were of the adjustable-rate variety. The interest rate was set for one month or one year at a time, resulting in the required mortgage payment to go up if and when interest rates went up.

Despite being ninjas, millions of families could no longer keep up with their increasing mortgage payments. As the housing boom slowed, home values stopped their furious increases. Consumers, lulled to sleep by the easy

2008

Mortgage and
Credit Crisis

The 2008
Election

credit, overextended themselves, buying second and third homes. As the party came to an end and the housing bubble burst, homeowners found themselves fucked and stuck and standing in long lines at the bank to turn in the keys to their now foreclosed home.

Fallout Boy

As the home-buying ninjas and other underqualified borrowers continued to default on their mortgages, institutions like Bear Stearns and Washington Mutual were forced to seek business partnerships with other nearly bankrupt entities to prevent themselves from going out of business. Major financial institutions reported losses of over $400 billion and climbing from the mortgage mess. The federal government, acting as the only entity large enough to do anything, injected $100 million into both Freddie Mac and Fannie Mae. Not to be outdone, Treasury Secretary Hank Paulson, along with Bernanke, pulled congressional strings in order to get Congress to pass a $700 billion bailout package to rescue lending institutions and prevent panic in our financial markets.

The lesson for Americans in all of this was simple; if you find a company that is willing to lend you more money than you can afford to pay back to buy a house that you ultimately cannot pay for, don't worry about the guilt, the federal government will square things up with the lender after you move out and find a larger more unaffordable home for you and your family.

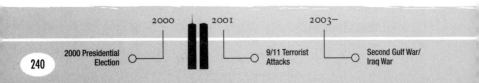

2000 — 2001 — 2003—

2000 Presidential Election — 9/11 Terrorist Attacks — Second Gulf War/ Iraq War

THE 2008 ELECTION

The opportunity to end the George W. circus

Opportunity of a Lifetime

As the world community celebrated George W. being removed from office through timely term limits, the leaders of the Democratic Party made plans to capitalize on the opportunity of following one of the most unpopular commanders in chief in American history. Not exactly admired for his openness, intellect, or public speaking abilities, President George W. Bush managed to inspire those who are supposed to hate him, hate him, and those who are supposed to like him on the basis of party affiliation also hate him.

With an unpopular war, high oil prices, a sluggish economy, and a lack of respect internationally, the voting electorate had November 4, 2008, circled and highlighted on every calendar they could find as a constant reminder of when the opportunity to end the George W. circus would present itself.

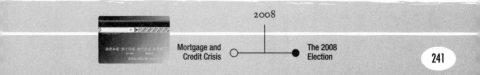

2008

Mortgage and
Credit Crisis

The 2008
Election

Let's Get This Party Started

For Democrats, there was no shortage of eager, constitutionally qualified candidates willing to make themselves available for the job. Those with a chance and those with no chance correctly filled out the required paperwork to have their name on the ballot for the Democratic Party nomination. By the time the registration deadline passed, nine Democrats from nine different states confidently declared themselves fit to lead the country in a new direction.

Joe Biden: Long time Delaware senator who enjoys both 7-Eleven and Dunkin Donuts despite the handicap of lacking an Indian from India accent. Capable driver but train enthusiast, he commutes from Delaware to Washington, D.C. by train every day. Odds of winning the nomination when he entered the race: a not so good 40,000 to 1.

Hillary Rodham Clinton: New York senator and former first lady. Known mostly as the woman who enjoyed watching her husband's impeachment hearing. She publicly admitted to accepting wild Bill's apology for getting some late-night oral action from the not-so-attractive white house intern, Monica Lewinsky. Clinton also enjoyed telling those who would listen how the marks on her back were battle scars from her failed health care initiative while first lady and not from any BDSM role-playing activities with her *it's hard to be faithful* husband. Odds of winning the nomination when she entered the race: a near lock at 5 to 2.

Christopher Dodd: Connecticut senator with overambitious goals. Meeting the criteria of being thirty-five years old, fourteen-year U.S. resident, and a natural-born citizen, Dodd seized the opportunity of having a chance at the Democratic nomination. Unfortunately, Dodd overlooked the fact that the primaries are a popularity contest, and in order to win people must

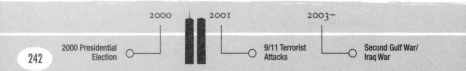

2000

2001

2003—

2000 Presidential Election

9/11 Terrorist Attacks

Second Gulf War/ Iraq War

like you. Dodd proved he was unpopular everywhere, most often receiving less than 1 percent of the vote. Even with optical scanner mishaps, Dodd proved to be perhaps the most unpopular of those believing they were fit to serve in the capacity of the president of the United States. Odds of winning the nomination when he entered the race: a time-wasting 3 million to 1.

John Edwards: Former ambulance-chasing attorney turned one-term U.S. senator. Known for $400 haircuts, this crusader for the poor gets by in his undersized 28,000-square-foot home on the outskirts of Chapel Hill, North Carolina. His political career took a shot to the sack when it was reported he had been enjoying some late-night banging with a woman not known to him as his wife. Odds of winning the nomination when he entered the race: an "I have a chance if I can come across sincere" 15 to 1.

Mike Gravel: Every once in a while you get a candidate who owes the American people an apology for taking up some of its time with their ridiculous desire to be president. As of today the electorate is waiting to hear "I'm sorry" from Gravel. Odds of winning the nomination when he entered the race: a Bill Gates 50 billion to 1.

Dennis Kucinich: First in the hearts of Frank and Virginia Kucinich is their three-times-married son Dennis Kucinich. Dennis received most of his support from white men who found his freakishly hot and out of place wife Elizabeth the perfect candidate for first lady after having to endure the unattractiveness of the two Bush first ladies of recent memory. Just before the filing deadline, Dennis woke up one morning with his naked wife lying next to him, and he figured he had beaten impossible odds before. Odds of winning the nomination when he entered the race: an unlikely nerd marrying a foreign hottie 500,000 to 1.

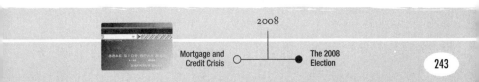

2008

Mortgage and
Credit Crisis

The 2008
Election

Barack Obama: The perfect American combination of half black, half white. Obama was blessed with his black father's Kenyan zeal for running great distances shoeless along with his white American mother's love of minorities. Known mostly for wanting to bring change we can believe in, this former community organizer campaigned on a platform of taking from the wealthy and giving to the larger voting population recognized as the middle class. Odds of winning the nomination when he entered the race: a not so good 75,000 to 1.

Bill Richardson: A Mexican descendent, ultimately done in by a "pay to play" scandal involving his campaign. Odds of winning the nomination when he entered the race: a dollar to peso exchange 1.25 million to 1.

Tom Vilsack: Yes, he made a mistake, and like Gravel, he owes America an apology for his whimsical attempt to become president. Odds of winning the nomination when he entered the race: a Gravel-like 50 billion to 1.

Republican Successors to the Throne

With a fully inspired Democratic field of candidates on record as wanting the job of top adversary to Russian President Dmitry Medvedev, Republicans of today and ghosts of the past bravely stood up in the face of the Bush/Cheney disaster and promised to provide four years of strange. Those making the leap included:

Sam Brownback: Kansas senator whose prolife stance for rape and incest got him the votes of the hard-core "life begins at conception and everyone should live prolife" wing of the Republican Party. Brownback ultimately enjoyed discouraging results in large part for his anti-Republican stance

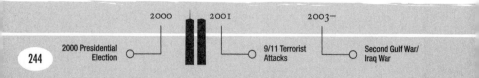

2000   2001   2003—

2000 Presidential Election

9/11 Terrorist Attacks

Second Gulf War/ Iraq War

on opening the borders and providing citizenship for millions and millions and millions and millions and millions and millions of illegal immigrants. Odds of winning the nomination when he entered the race: a "you must not be serious" 750,000 to 1.

Jim Gilmore: Former governor of Virginia. He may not have been the first one in the race, but he was the first one out of the race. Gilmore disqualified himself for not being electable. Odds of winning the nomination when he entered the race: an "O.J. Simpson was innocent of the Brentwood double murders" 76.5 million to 1.

Rudy Giuliani: Former New York City mayor, he was praised for his handling of the 9/11 attacks. Early front-runner Giuliani lacked porn-star staying power as his lead faltered, he released quickly, subsequently quitting the race. Frequently marrying, Giuliani keeps a list of 400 guests who remain on call at all times for his next wedding. Odds of winning the nomination when he entered the race: a near Hillary-like 9 to 2.

Mike Huckabee: Former Southern Baptist minister turned overweight Arkansas governor. Fearing death by heart attack, he lost 110 pounds, or one Katie Holmes. The Huck struggled to get over the hump of his wife having far too many Barbara Bush physical features. After being described as both gregarious and loquacious, most Americans figured he had a dueling terminal illnesses and thought maybe running for president was on his "bucket list." It has been speculated that if he and Kucinich's wife were a marital item he may have received the Republican nomination. Odds of winning the nomination when he entered the race: a shot-in-the-dark 625,000 to 1.

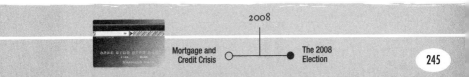

2008

Mortgage and Credit Crisis

The 2008 Election

Duncan Hunter: Representative from California. Did not drop out as quickly as Gilmore but probably should have. Odds of winning the nomination when he entered the race: a hell-freezing-over 4.5 million to 1.

Alan Keyes: After inadvertently marking the wrong box on his party affiliation form, Keyes became the first black member of the Republican Party. He hoped to quickly parlay his notoriety into the nomination. Doesn't he know Republican is old Latin for "Whites Only"? Odds of winning the nomination when he entered the race: a "he's even blacker than Barack!" 50 billion to 1.

John McCain: The nearly dead senator from Arizona broke out the straight-talk express to capture the nomination that was stolen from him back in 2000 when the George W. camp resorted to slander. Referencing his time at the "Hanoi Hilton" during his prisoner of war stage, McCain capitalized on America's sympathy for his wartime struggles and for his fortuitous marrying of a sexy and wealthy beer distributor heir. Odds of winning the nomination when he entered the race: an "in it to win it" 50 to 1.

Ron Paul: The feisty and frustrated representative from Texas was left on the outside looking in from the beginning. Despite the obvious generation gap, Paul's strongest support came from young weekend-binge-drinking college students. Odds of winning the nomination when he entered the race: a perfect beer pong season 900,000 to 1.

Mitt Romney: Former Massachusetts governor, he enjoyed the challenge of spending tens of millions of dollars of his own money in an effort to overcome his Mormon anchor. Americans pondered, "which one of his wives would be considered the First Lady?" Odds of winning the

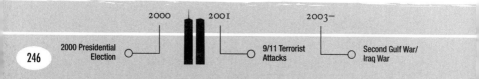

2000   2001   2003—

2000 Presidential Election

9/11 Terrorist Attacks

Second Gulf War/ Iraq War

nomination when he entered the race: a "Catholic Church advocating for polygamy" 150,000 to 1.

Tom Tancredo: As suspected, his Republican nomination bid was simply a bad joke that got out of hand. Odds of winning the nomination when he entered the race: a long-shot-at-best 10 million to 1.

Fred Thompson: Suffering from dementia, he wandered off the set of *Law and Order* unsupervised and into the Republican primary. He pointed out that Flomax keeps him peeing regularly, not excessively, which was enough for him to receive medical clearance to perform the job of commander in chief. Odds of winning the nomination when he entered the race: a "*Law and Order* winning best comedy" 3,500 to 1.

Tommy Thompson: He was just fucking kidding, or at least Republican voters thought so, as his candidacy was completely unnecessary. Odds of winning the nomination when he entered the race: a humorous 7.5 million to 1.

The After Party

As more and more candidates realized how unpopular they were with the American people, the field narrowed to old man McCain on the center right for the Republicans and the biracial Obama on the left of left for the Democrats. Hillary Clinton, the presumptive Democratic nominee, was left questioning if she really was the first lady to the first black president as nearly everyone, regardless of complexion, voted for Obama.

With their respective nominations secured, the two polar-opposite candidates scheduled less than elaborate press conferences to announce their vice presidential running mates. Obama shocked the electorate with his choice of

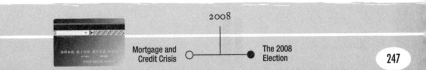

an old white guy and former primary foe, Delaware Senator Joe "if my lips are moving there is a good chance I am going to offend someone, mostly likely a minority," Biden. With Biden attending Catholic church, the Obama camp prayed that priests would keep their hands out of the altar boys' pants until after election day.

☞ *As for McCain, he took his strategic advisors to the early bird at his favorite Arizona diner to pick his running mate.* ☜ The squash casserole must have been extra special that night, as McCain went with a far more traditional choice in a moose-hunting hockey mom and current governor of Alaska, Sarah Palin. The rifle-using, big-game-killing governor was as comfortable in her designer lumberjack jacket and orange crossing-guard vest as she was in the $180,000 worth of Neiman Marcus clothes she purchased with Republican campaign funds to make her sexier and more physically appealing than her male counterpart. With their sidekicks chosen, it was time to vote!

Election Day

The media was amped for Election Day. For months, speculation had been running wild about whether or not the young and probably not yet qualified Democrat from Illinois could pull off the ultimate upset. ☞ *As for the seventy-two-year-old Republican hopeful, John McCain, by the time the polls closed on the West Coast at 8:00 p.m. PST, he had been asleep for two hours.* ☜ Campaign aides awoke him to let him know that he received millions more votes than anyone could have imagined just a few short months ago. Unfortunately, even with his better-than-expected showing, Obama rocked the vote, winning the popular and electoral vote handily.

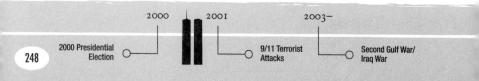

2000
2001
2003—

2000 Presidential Election

9/11 Terrorist Attacks

Second Gulf War/ Iraq War

All in all, 131,237,603 American adults oddly enough exercised their right not to have another white man join the other white men who had earned the distinction to lead as the president of the United States. To celebrate his historic victory, Obama invited 250,000 of his closest friends, including the enlarging Oprah Winfrey, to join him at Grant Park in Chicago, Illinois. With video of his acceptance speech beaming around the world, it was official: Barack Obama had the kind of change he could believe in.

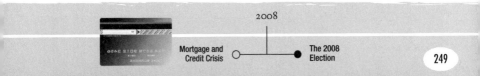

2008

Mortgage and
Credit Crisis

The 2008
Election

THE SLACKER'S GUIDE TO U.S. HISTORY FINAL EXAM

They say that those who do not learn history are doomed to repeat it. If that involved repeating JFK's life, there would be many volunteers, right up until the whole shooting situation. To that end, please test your knowledge of U.S. history by completing the following exam:

Questions

1. This civil rights leader was shot dead while he stood outside on a second story balcony at the less than classy Lorraine Motel.

2. The United States' favorite adulterer

3. Her unique ability to sit and do nothing changed civil rights forever.

4. He traded oil for virgins.

5. Re-enactment of Prohibition would kill this city's tourism.

6. This Minnesota congressman nearly kept Ted Kennedy sober.

7. Did this All-American half-African win an historic election? YES HE DID.

8. His nickname makes you wonder if he could tie his Johnson in a knot.

   _____

9. The French lent us assistance in the form of equipment and purple silk vests for this war.

   _____

10. The pseudo-intellectual friend of Mother Earth

   _____

11. This family had a hard-on for a desert oasis not named Las Vegas.

   _____

12. Think hard: Who is our most forgettable president?

   _____

13. This president enjoyed slave-girl action at his Mount Vernon estate.

   _____

14. These people were kind enough to volunteer to relocate to a less desirable location to make room for us.

   _____

15. He was an icon for young Southern boys who enjoyed wearing bed sheets.

   _____

16. She was an underage Indian bride.

   _____

17. Much to his dread, the court ruled he was not even a person, but property.

   _____

18. If your best friend breaks up with his girlfriend it is _____ for you to begin dating her after three months.

   _____

19. Who was so hard up he went door-to-door in the middle of the night?

   _____

20. The settlers to this lost colony were mostly likely lured inland for hot and spicy Anglo-Indian love and then never heard from again.

_____

21. Canadian-born porn star

_____

22. America joined this organization so Luxembourg would protect us.

_____

23. This war saw 2.8 million age-qualified American men have their name pulled from the draft hat.

_____

24. This former Secretary of State purchased the polar bear playground of Alaska for 1.9 cents an acre.

_____

25. Sympathizer to the poor Franklin D. Roosevelt signed the Fair Labor Standards Act into law, requiring American workers to receive a get-rich-quick wage of at least _____ an hour for their time and effort while at work

_____

Answers

1. Martin Luther King, Junior
2. JFK
3. Rosa Parks
4. Saddam Hussein
5. Las Vegas
6. Volstead
7. Obama
8. Tricky Dick Nixon
9. Revolutionary
10. Gore
11. Bush
12. McKinley
13. Washington
14. Indians
15. Davis
16. Sacagawea
17. Dred Scott
18. Kosher
19. Paul Revere
20. Roanoke
21. Towers
22. NATO
23. World War I
24. William Seward
25. 25 cents

INDEX

About the Slackers

The authors' back-story is littered with empty beer cans, outrageous stunts, and an enthusiasm for making people laugh. College friends, roommates, and fraternity brothers, they headed into the real world after chickening out on a magazine venture in their twenties. One chose the predictable safety of a bi-weekly paycheck courtesy of corporate America, and the other chose to grab a seat on the unpredictable roller coaster ride sponsored by entrepreneurship. They got married, fertilized their wife's eggs a couple of times, and continued to enrich their long-standing friendship by circling back and creating comically informative books, of which this is the first.

Art Credits

Bathtub © 2009 Jupiterimages Corporation
Tampons © 2009 Jupiterimages Corporation
Beer bottle © 2009 Jupiterimages Corporation
Beer can © 2009 Jupiterimages Corporation
Spur © 2009 Jupiterimages Corporation
Gloves © 2009 Jupiterimages Corporation
Sexy woman © 2009 Jupiterimages Corporation
High heel © 2009 Jupiterimages Corporation
Truck © 2009 Jupiterimages Corporation
Twin towers © 2009 Jupiterimages Corporation
Sombrero © 2009 Jupiterimages Corporation
Ball and chain © 2009 Jupiterimages Corporation
Bomb © 2009 Jupiterimages Corporation
Cat © 2009 Jupiterimages Corporation
Moon © 2009 Jupiterimages Corporation
Going Out Of Business sign © Ken Brown/123RF
Teabag © Ahmet Ihsan Ariturk /123RF
Bible © M.G. Mooij/123RF
$500 © peterdenovo/123RF
Parental advisory © Dan Talson/123RF
Hunting vest © Blaj Gabriel/123RF
GPS © John Tomaselli/123RF
Credit card © hakakatb/123RF
Vodka bottle © Dmitry Kudryavtsev/123RF
Thong © Vaidas Bucys/123RF